# The 30 Teachings of Mary Magdalene:
## How to Advance Your Soul

ISBN: 978-1-4525-4689-6 (sc)
ISBN: 978-1-4525-4688-9 (e)
Balboa Press books may be ordered through booksellers or by contacting:

Balboa Press
A Division of Hay House
1663 Liberty Drive
Bloomington, IN 47403
www.balboapress.com
1-(877) 407-4847

Because of the dynamic nature of the Internet, any web addresses or
links contained in this book may have changed since publication and
may no longer be valid. The views expressed in this work are solely those
of the author and do not necessarily reflect the views of the publisher,
and the publisher hereby disclaims any responsibility for them.

The author of this book does not dispense medical advice or prescribe the use
of any technique as a form of treatment for physical, emotional, or medical
problems without the advice of a physician, either directly or indirectly. The
intent of the author is only to offer information of a general nature to help
you in your quest for emotional and spiritual well-being. In the event you use
any of the information in this book for yourself, which is your constitutional
right, the author and the publisher assume no responsibility for your actions.

Any people depicted in stock imagery provided by Thinkstock are models,
and such images are being used for illustrative purposes only.
Certain stock imagery © Thinkstock.

Printed in the United States of America

Balboa Press rev. date: 4/27/2012

# The 30 Teachings of Mary Magdalene: How to Advance Your Soul

*Eva Rose*

**BALBOA.**
PRESS

A DIVISION OF HAY HOUSE

# Endorsement:

"I know that this book will make a significant impact on the world, transforming the hearts and minds of all who come into contact with it. The 30 teachings really touched me and I experienced definite shifts after reading them. Somehow, Magdalene's words are charged with a powerful frequency pertaining to our soul's evolution. Her message is meant to help us all evolve more gracefully and consciously."

~Shanell Vaughn

ALSO BY EVA ROSE

A Guide for Advancing Your Soul

For my daughter, Jordyn.
May you be blessed to walk this human journey
graced with the spirit of Magdalene to guide your way.

# ACKNOWLEDGEMENTS

Thank you to my family.
This work would not have come into existence
without your unconditional love and patience.
You have gifted me the time, space and privacy that
I needed to travel this journey.
I will always be grateful.

# INTRODUCTION

## The Story before this Book

AS A way of inviting you into the journey ahead, I would briefly like to share with readers the relevant experiences that brought this book into existence. Before this book came to be, I was quite content in my life with much to be grateful for. I had a loving family, a satisfying career, a few good friends, plenty of privacy, and a small financial cushion to sit on when I needed some down time. I can remember the feeling of contentment because I had specifically created a comfort zone for my life and even a rather neat and tidy box to fit it all into. Yes, my plan for my life felt adequate.

Then something happened. I began having recurring lucid dreams. Almost every night for three years as I slept I was being chased. First spiders then snakes relentlessly pursued me. Waking visions also haunted me and I fought to balance my growing fear and confusion with the certainty that these occurrences were very real and happening for a reason. The experiences within these dreams intensified over time as they came closer and closer until the night I was finally bitten.

It was true that this awakening had tried to happen at other times in my life. Two separate near death experiences at the ages of four and eight had both permitted an opening for me to glimpse the truth behind the veil. But both times I had somehow managed to close the door again, just in time to ignore the message that Spirit was sharing.

Thirty years later, surrendering to a higher plan was still not anywhere on my agenda. But it was becoming painfully obvious that something beyond my conscious comprehension was still trying to get my attention again. I attempted to ignore it again, endeavoring to squeeze myself back into that box. I even popped out two ribs during this time period. Talk about your body manifesting what your mind isn't ready to wrap itself around! My chiropractor was even flummoxed, finally suggesting that perhaps an adjustment in my life was needed instead to bring me into alignment. I now understand that my ribs were just a reminder of how I would feel if I decided to climb back in that box I had outgrown. It was like they were saying to me: "You want to stick to your plan? Okay, but it's going be pretty uncomfortable from this point forth."

Shortly after being bitten by a snake in the crescendo of my recurring dream, I released my resistance. And in an instant I was being carried over from the ordinary into the extraordinary.

# Your Guide for the Journey

MARY MAGDALENE first introduced herself to me by way of a spontaneous encounter while I was driving to my daughter's school one afternoon. She shared the assignment and asked if I would trust her to be my guide in completing a specific task. Once I realized that this was actually happening, I became willing to suspend my own disbelief, and agreed to follow her instructions step by step on what turned out to be a miraculous month long journey into the heart of 30 sacred teachings.

Before this encounter, I knew very little about Mary Magdalene or her historical significance. Throughout my adult life I would call myself a spiritual seeker with deep personal beliefs about who I am and the meaning of why I am here. I have, however kept my personal spiritual beliefs quite private overall, so I could not have been more surprised when the events that led me to this material took place.

Shortly after Magdalene introduced herself, I woke up in the middle of the night with a very strong urge to write in my journal. I sat in my bed at 3am with pen in hand, but nothing came. I was about to give up on the urge when something happened.

Without forethought, I wrote the numbers 1-30 down the side of the page in my journal and starting at the first number I began a list. This went on for a few minutes until the list was complete. I sat and reviewed what had been written and wondered to myself what the list meant. I heard the following response and wrote it down word for word exactly as I heard it:

≈

"You are ready to embark on the path of embracing your own divinity to advance your soul. We will offer 30 teachings for the journey by way of inspiration. Each of these will come forth in the time and with the experiences you need to understand the meaning of the teachings and integrate them into your being. The wording of the teachings is exact and they will come to you in the order that you will be ready to experience them. Once they have all been revealed, you will offer them to others who are also ready to consciously embark on their own divine journey. You will be shown the way."

≈

For the next four weeks while each of the teachings were revealed, I lived in a state of continuous penetrating joy. I found them to be timeless and similar to the essential teachings of all great spiritual disciplines, revealing deep universal truths about our own souls and the reason we are here traveling this human journey. One by one, they uncover ways to raise human consciousness, how to receive direct access to Source, the true purpose of relationships, and much more. The culmination of the teachings speaks to two planes of divine realization: how to personally experience the divine within, and also how to raise your soul's consciousness while performing your earthly tasks.

Magdalene offered specific ways for me to record the teachings and I began by taking dictation longhand in a journal. Within a few days I used a voice recorder as a more efficient tool to capture her exact words that were coming through directly.

Her teachings are written here in the exact order in which they were received and the words within them are substantially unchanged. From my personal experience and of others who have internalized this wisdom, it is suggested that Magdalene's words carry a unique frequency and after reading them one can feel an internal shift taking place.

The complete story of my personal journey that led me to the teachings can be found in my book, *A Guide for Advancing Your Soul*, which also offers tools to integrate these teachings into a daily spiritual practice. This manuscript was created both as a companion to the complete book and is also designed as a stand-alone for those who desire the purity of Magdalene's words that were captured within her 30 sacred teachings.

We are all living in a period of global spiritual evolution, when great numbers of people are also seeking knowledge on how to accelerate and magnify their evolvement personally. By following each teaching with Magdalene as your guide, you will have everything necessary to consciously embark on your own powerful journey of advancing your soul.

Your Messenger,

*Eva Rose.*

# The Way Home

All this talk of peace and bliss!
My path is more of my ego's uprising,
burning in revolution to remain in charge.
Without separate and alone who am I?
Is this discontent a case of mistaken identity?

Through screams and wails of shredding fear,
I am dragged towards the revealing dawn.
Grasping backward into the rubble I scratch and cling
to my old cloak of flawed and broken parts.
But the humbled façade of who I was begins to
smolder in the wreckage, turning ego's illusions into ash.

In exhausted surrender, I finally release my grip and tumble
onto the doorstep of Union.
I exhale, permitting myself to take rest
in the Divine still water.
I open my weary eyes to witness my own reflection
in God's shining grace.
I am home.

Eva Rose

# THE 30 TEACHINGS OF MARY MAGDALENE

1. Expand Your Horizon
2. Devote Time in Nature
3. Always Place Self First
4. Walk Your Own Path
5. Live in Faith
6. Open Your Heart
7. Master Your Mind
8. Keep Your Feet Firmly Planted
9. Remain a Humble Servant
10. Accept Abundance
11. Tread Lightly on Mother Earth
12. Reveal Thy Self
13. Enter into Sacred Relationship
14. Connect to Source
15. Know You Are the Miracle
16. Be Thankful
17. Call on Your Support Team
18. Trust the Source
19. Let Your Feelings Inform Your Path
20. Become Watchful for Earthly Signals
21. Accept the Winds of Change
22. Gather the Tools for Your Trade
23. Bless the Challenges
24. Go Where You Are Called
25. Practice Non-Attachment
26. Maintain Balance
27. Breathe In the Aroma of Creation
28. Express Yourself
29. Remember We Are One
30. Go Silently Within

# Teaching 1:
# Expand Your Horizon

**"It's a brilliant surface in that sunlight.
The horizon seems quite close to you
because the curvature is so much
more pronounced than here on earth.
It's an interesting place to be.
I recommend it."**

**Neil Armstrong**

WE COME together to offer the memory of what has been lost in humanity's history and what must be returned in order for the new era of peace on Planet Earth. We will work with you to bring forth both the heavenly wisdom and Mother Earth's planetary wisdom for it is time to remember that you are divine beings traveling an earthly journey with divinity as your destiny. And we begin our time together with this first teaching for how to recognize your soul so that you may know your divinity: Expand your Horizon.

Expand the horizon of who you currently believe yourself to be. Whatever you believe yourself to be, you are truly so much more. Many of you have been bound by limited thoughts and visions. Your true greatness does not understand earthly limitation. Humanity has defined artificial limits on infinite beings and this is the counterintuitive irony you all live with. Remaining small serves no true purpose and is not the way to your divinity. No one ever made a difference from living inside a box. Be bold. Break free from the confined existence that no longer serves you or the life you came here to live.

The horizon of the soul is vast and radiant. You can choose to experience this exquisite beauty in human form. Do not wait to return to Spirit to remember who you truly are. Begin to expand your horizon by making a commitment. Commit to embracing your divinity and your world will become limitless. Walk the path of the Divine. I will show you the way. And So It Is.

# Teaching 2:
# Devote Time in Nature

"I went to the woods
because I wished to live deliberately,
and not, when I came to die,
discover that I had not lived."

Henry David Thoreau

ASK FOR permission to enter nature. Pay attention to your surroundings. You are safe. Tread lightly and in reverence, as you are a guest. Nature is the most natural place for you to be. Nature is the place where many will find for the first time, or be reintroduced to their spirit and connect to the Divine Source. One only has to turn their face in the direction of the sun's rays to remember the feeling of Source's energy. The breath of life is breathed more deeply when you breathe in the scents of nature. Allow time for your feet to tread on the grounds that are not sealed by concrete.

Allow time in your days to take a seat on a rock instead of a plastic chair and feel the earth beneath you. Nature has much to share and welcomes you into her home. Nature says to you all: "Do not lock the doors of your homes so tightly. Open your doors and let the breeze blow through your halls. And from time to time, allow the wind to call your name outside the doors that confine you."

Enter into Her home to observe and be in reverence of Her perfection. And after a time you shall come to a knowing, that the vastness of life and all of the experiences available to you are inside your buildings. It grows beyond, within petals of flowers and on the feet of bees. It grows the bird's feathers and takes rest on the breeze. It grows in the sunlight with the help of rain, and inside of you, where Spirit calls your name.

And So It Is.

# Teaching 3:
# Always Place Self First

**"Self-love is the source of all our other loves."**

**Pierre Corneille**

ALWAYS PLACE self first. Many of you believe that acting on this statement would be an act of selfishness when it is truly an act of self-care. To truly know who you are, you must first become your own priority. If you are waiting for another to place you first at the head of your own line, you may be waiting for quite some time. If all of the hours in your day are spent on activities other than yourself, you are stating to the Universe that you do not matter. And you do matter. You in fact matter far more than you can realize from the perspective you have there in the earthly realm. Placing self first is a statement that you know that you matter and are showing up for this task of life and are ready to serve.

A moment on how you can begin to incorporate this teaching. Spend sacred time in solitude daily. You may wish to begin by spending a short time each day without the noise and distractions of life to just sit quietly alone and be still. Mornings are a good time for quiet solitude before the bustle of the day takes over. This practice will allow the static of the mind to dissipate. It doesn't take long. You have the time, you are just afraid to take it. Don't allow the excuses to distract you. There is enough time to do it all. Taking time alone is how you will become at ease with all that unfolds throughout each day and all those that drain and pull at your energy system. Your mind and body will become balanced, compassionate, and centered with those around you when you first spend time in solitude.

Service of others requires service to self, for without the self being cared for your service to others will be forsaken of your best abilities. The word "Always" in the title of this teaching is intentional and essential to grasp the importance of this teaching. Becoming your first priority will give you enough time and energy to accomplish everything you wish.

You will notice that not only will you have enough time; you will also increase your energy with the practice of self first. You will become plentiful and boundless with your energy. If you practice this only sometimes or once in a while, you are treating yourself as a wilted plant. The idea of placing self first at any time will be a challenge for some and doing so all the time will seem near impossible to many. But let us be clear that this teaching is not one that can be rearranged or passed over. Without practicing this teaching each day, truly embracing your divinity will be folly.

And So It Is.

# Teaching 4:
# Walk Your Own Path

"Do not go where the path may lead,
go instead where there is no
path and leave a trail."

**Ralph Waldo Emerson**

IT IS time to walk your own path in life. You must begin to take up space. You deserve to be here. Walking on the sidelines of life will not get you very far. When you see others walking their path do not immediately yield to them, their desires, their needs, their footprint, their space. Walk your path, regardless of who else is walking around you, or even in front of you. There is no need to yield; there is room enough for both. Your path is unique to you and for you. Yielding, walking on the edge of the path, walking another's pace, or another's path all together will not serve you. Walk in the center of the path.

Also remain centered on your path without changing course or yielding when you are faced with the opinion of others. They may judge you, scorn you and even become determined to shove you off your path. They are just in fear. They have yet to remember their own grandness. Do not be concerned with how it looks or what others are thinking of you. Let them look. They are not on your path. And you are not on theirs. If they ask why you walk the path in your own way, simply tell them: "This is where I choose to be. It is my choice."

It is also important to know your natural rhythm and speed and follow that. If you speed up in haste for fear you are blocking another's pace, do not. You will lose your wind and become tired. If you slow down because you think or fear you may be moving too fast for yourself, do not. Your own pace will energize you and keep you vital.

Let us also share about walking the path of convention. You must walk a path that is different from the one you were told to walk by others or you won't make a lasting difference and your footprints won't be remembered. The conventional path will keep you as sheep amongst the herd, all doing the same thing, drinking from the same trough, ingesting the same grass, wandering the same hills. Convention says you must all be the same and just follow directions. This is the path of the least risk. It will not allow for you to stand out and share the unique soul that you came here to be. Quiet the voices of others inside your head and only and always listen to your own.

And while walking the path of your own soul, allow others the same freedom. When you see another's journey or action or way of living, and you disagree with their choices, simply say, "It is their journey, not mine." Do not speak words of judgment or opinion. Stand back from their path with love in your heart and your ego on the shelf. Do not block their way. Allow others their journey, their lessons, their experiences, their life.

Interference is one of the most disrespectful acts one can do to another's journey. It houses a much lower vibration and does not resonate with any part of your soul. If you create it for long enough it will manifest as illness inside your body. Toxic relationships that do not serve the good of all that enter into them will create a lower vibration and manifest illness because it blocks the path of spirit manifesting. Illness resonates with interference. That is what illness is and it moves against the natural rhythm.

To block one's path in any way without being invited is the definition of injury. Many who interfere hold the false belief that they are just being helpful. The act of interference is not helpful. It is unkind and comes from your ego that is driven there by fear.

When you notice yourself wanting to block the path of another, be it with words, thoughts of judgment, or an action, pause and ask yourself one question: "What am I so afraid of in this moment that I am willing to cause injury to another?" The first response you hear to this question will be your truth speaking. Do not toss it away, even if you dislike what you hear. Allow the response to inform you and step aside. Move yourself back to your own path and concentrate your energy and time there.

There are very few instances when intervention or interference is truly required when you are witnessing the path of another. For instance, small children need to be guided and protected, but not hovered over. When you hover, you are acting out of fear or to meet your own needs.

How do you know when you are hovering? You will find yourself standing so close you are breathing in their energy field, energetically, and sometimes even physically. Step back and allow them to walk their own path. A flower that has been trodden on cannot bloom. Allow them their natural expression and do not stomp on their true nature and sprit. As they grow with age and maturity, continuously take steps back. They need your guidance, and the guidance of others, but not for very long, and not as much guidance as some of you may believe.

While watching them grow, always be inclusive of their good opinion, and ask them often, what would they choose so that they may practice their natural right of free will and choice? Take these responses under real consideration before deciding anything on their behalf. They matter. Listen to them. Only block or protect when truly necessary, when they are in danger for their life, or when something occurs that would cause permanent damage on their path. And then set them free to walk on their chosen path.

And when you set them free, release them in reverence. The only two things you have more of than your children is experiences and time in this incarnation. You are otherwise, equals with your children. They are not yours. They only came through you to receive the unique circumstances, experiences, and gifts that you have to offer them in preparation for their journey. Offer them the tools they will need to walk their own path. Place those that they want to use in their backpack, and then release them. And from that time of release when they begin to walk their own paths, restrain from opinion, interference, and even support unless you are expressly invited. This is how to walk your own path in this divine life.

And So It Is.

# Teaching 5:
# Live In Faith

**"Faith in oneself is the best and safest course."**

**Michelangelo**

AT THE beginning of each day, spend a few moments of your time in quiet meditation and reflection. Be in reverence of your commitment to your path. This is a journey of faith. This is what it feels like to not only be in faith for a moment or an hour, but to walk a journey of faith-full living.

This is the Initiation of Faith. Don't bring fear on the journey. Fear and faith cannot occupy the same space at once. Become conscious of when you come into contact with fear; fear that you feel, and fear that you see in a variety of forms with others around you. When you notice fear in others, practice sending them a blessing of love. This is the practice of a truly divine being. When you notice that you have chosen a state of fear within yourself, encircle yourself in a circle of love with the intention of restoring your faith. Then with each breath, breathe faith into your body and release your fear as you exhale. Continue this practice until you feel the fear dissipate and dissolve.

Nothing is accidental. It has all been in preparation for Now. Just remember to have faith for it is required on any journey worth taking. And your journey will require you to walk outside of your comfort zone. Now, be still and breathe in God's faith in you.

And So It Is.

# Teaching 6:
# Open Your Heart

**"Go to you bosom: Knock there,
and ask your heart what it doth know."**

**William Shakespeare**

TODAY WE offer an initiation for the heart. We have come to remind you that you are love. You were made from love and will return to love. And you are here on this human journey to remember that you are a divine creation, and therefore you are love incarnate. It is one and the same.

Journey to your heart and expand your love from there. Love knows where to flow. All it needs is for you to allow the wave of love to enter and flow through your heart. It was always there, you just have to reawaken and expand it. Breathe love in, and practice this statement as you breathe: "I am a divine being of love breathing love into myself, and I also share love with all those I meet on my path today."

As your love expands with each breath through your heart allow it to wash over your entire divine being. Once you have flowed love into yourself, then flow this wave outwards to share it with all those you meet on your path. See the love then expand beyond your own vision and out into the heart of the universe.

Use the visualization of this wave of love to pour through you at all times, and especially during times that you may forget your true self and who you are. Connect with this energy; as it is with you always. You are love. Your soul knows this truth.

Serve yourself and also others with the abundant wave of love. This practice will dissolve your fears, dissolve your depression, and begin to dissolve your ego. This practice will make room in your heart for forgiveness; forgiveness for self and forgiveness for all. This practice will also energize your being and increase your vibration with divine consciousness.

With this practice you will come to remember that all is one and the way is love. The past, present and future are truly all beating at once within the universal heart of now. You are cycling in it at all times, and this practice of love with your heart will dissolve away your old story and invite in the abundance of now, the truth for what you are doing here, for who you are being here, and of who you have always been.

Today you have awakened your heart. Visit your divine heart and practice flowing this powerful wave of love through yourself without conditions. It will help to bring ease, balance, and intelligence to the mind.

And So It Is.

# Teaching 7:
# Master Your Mind

"One must first discipline and
control one's own mind.
If a man can control his mind
he can find the way to Enlightenment,
and all wisdom and virtue will
naturally come to him."

**Buddha**

TODAY WE offer an initiation for the mind. The heart and the mind need to be in balance in order to be enlightened. Overusing the mind will throw you out of balance. Being out of balance with the heart will do the same. The heart informs the mind, as the mind informs the heart. This is why they have been given to you for your human journey, for both are needed and are gifts to be used together. That is the key to the full experience of being a sacred and powerful being. If one is closed, the other is over used and you will not be able flow in full frequency.

Today is about learning how to calm and train the thoughts of the mind so that your heart and mind can come into balance. Some of you like to move from thought directly into action without passing through the heart. We have shown you how to open the heart and today we must begin training the mind.

The process is simple. The key to the process is a quiet mind. Sit and be still. Do no-thing and peace of mind will come. The voice of the Universal Soul cannot be heard clearly amidst your constant chatter. This chatter comes from the ego, which does not like to be silenced. Have the ego step aside. The mind will then calm and quiet down, allowing the Divine to inform.

We are with you more clearly when you first take the time to clear the mind of ego's clutter, of external circumstance, of earthly troubles, of past and future worries. Watch the thoughts pass and then release them. It only takes willingness to be breathe, then be still. With each breath you are slowing down the mind. From there you will be able to connect to the Divine and tune into the frequency of the Source of your own soul. Listen to my words:

> I find my center in my body and I begin to breathe.
> In each breath I breathe more slowly,
> I hear quiet come over me.
> I see the waters of my mind,
> the breeze now blows more gently.
> The rippling waters of my mind now fade into serenity.
> One word then fills the inner spaces
> Until all that remains is….Still.

And So It Is.

# Teaching 8:
# Keep your Feet Firmly Planted

"Each blade of grass has its spot on earth whence it draws its life, its strength; and so is man rooted to the land from which he draws his faith together with his life."

Joseph Conrad

WE OFFER you our next teaching on how to keep your feet firmly planted while walking your earthly journey. This is important, because you are of both heaven and earth and you must keep your feet firmly planted as you walk between both worlds. Notice how you plant your feet. How do you stand? How do you feel in your body? Your feet are the memory keepers of the Earth's energy.

To maintain the connection with Mother Earth take care of your feet and the "soles" of your feet. It is not by chance that your feet are connected to the word, "sole." Walk often without shoes. Put your feet directly on the earth and do this often. It will help to ground you to your physical home and your physical world. You will be reminded of this when you physically connect your feet with Mother Earth.

When you are off course spiritually, the Universe will show you by blocking your physical path. These blocks and closed doors that you experience are the nudge so that you may pay attention and perhaps make a course correction. Some of you wait for a fog horn to sound in your ear before you choose to correct your course. It is always your choice. But with your feet planted, you will be able to correct your course in a timely fashion.

You must also plant your feet firmly on the Mother Earth for the benefit of your physical well-being. Neglecting the body will not allow you to spend time being, because when the physical body is ill it is a distraction to being able to listen to the heavenly guidance. Illness in the physical body is also one of your greatest teachers in the physical realm. It is a very loud wake up call; an alarm so to speak. Illness is there to tell you that you are off course and/or out of balance. If your physical body is ill, you have lost your spiritual balance.

The food you ingest is another way to keep your feet planted. Ingesting clean food in a conscious way will assist your overall journey. Sending your food a simple blessing of thanks will assist your body by increasing the vibration of the food. You can simply state "Thank you food for coming into my body and providing me now with nourishment and energy in order for me to complete my tasks on this day." As you increase your vibrational energies you will need less quantities of food and you may experience true physical hunger less frequently. This is natural. You are running more effective energies through your vehicle and literally burning cleaner fuel. You will require less to operate your vehicle, less food, less sleep, and certainly less chemicals.

You also may be spending time ingesting toxins that do not serve you. You will become more sensitive to toxins that alter your body and your mind as your vibrational energies increase. These chemicals take you out of your body and your mind. That is why some of you ingest them, because you don't want to be here, in-bodied. We understand that suffering can feel like it is too much at times. These substances are only delaying your ability to transform since they take you off your true course. It becomes more difficult to remember who you really are and what your path is when these toxic chemicals are present. The word 'present' here is an irony of words because toxins in fact act upon your body and mind to distract you from being present. Spending less time ingesting toxic chemicals will speed the recovery of your mind and body, bringing you back to center, and remembering your path and who you are. It will increase the speed and lightness of your journey.

Other forms of toxins include spending time in the "presence" of toxic physical beings that are not in harmony with who you are. Pay attention to your body every day for it is the keeper of your soul. Again, it is the vehicle that allows you to manifest in the physical realm. Treat it as the sacred tool it is, and it will serve you in wellness.

You will notice the one thing that you ingest that you will need more of is water. One of the key ways to keep your body physically well is to hydrate with water. Your earthly body is mostly water and requires more that you think to operate smoothly. Bless the water that you take into your body and it will vibrate to match the frequency that your body needs to be in optimal condition. Spending time in salt water from our oceans will be a conductor for you to connect with your spirit. When you need to recharge your physical batteries, or if you are feeling disconnected from your Source place your body in water. It is a simple task and will work for and with you.

Another generator for the physical body to keep your feet planted is the breath. Shallow breathers tend to be ill more often that those who breathe more deeply. Shallow breathers have practiced this in order to disconnect from their heart, and the practice of shallow breathing will do that for them. Shallow breathers tend to house more fear in their bodies and minds. The opposite and conscious practice of deep breathing will keep you firmly connected to body and physical wellness. Deep breathing will also serve as a conduit of connecting to Source and higher levels of consciousness. It will extend and expand your physical life. The breath of life is called that on purpose.

Notice your own breath and where you allow it to come into your body. Is it in the area of the chest, or the inner core (your belly area.) Practicing bringing breath all the way down into the core will connect you more deeply to the heavens while bringing you into earthly alignment. Also notice how you breathe in and out when taking a deep breath. If the inhale is shorter in duration than the exhale, you tend to give less to yourself and more to others. This is out of balance. And the opposite is also true. A longer inhale and noticeably shorter exhale, you tend to give more to yourself and less to others. Just notice what the duration of your breath tells you, and by practicing breathing you can come into balance and equalize the breath of life.

When your feet are firmly planted on Mother Earth you will receive even more benefits, such as your intuition will be stronger. Those beings that are not tethered to the Earth and float above their bodies and their feet don't truly touch the ground are less connected to their intuition (In To It). This brings the opportunity for more accidents, mishaps, and physical injury to your vehicle. It also makes it more challenging for the heart to connect in relationship to others in a meaningful way. When your feet are firmly planted you can access and hear your intuitive voice more readily and also avoid accidents and injury. You can also learn your lessons at a faster pace so that you can get on with the business of your purpose here.

Another advantage of these grounding abilities that plant your feet will be your ability to read the energy of a room or a person with ease and accuracy. You will know the relationships you have encountered or entered into that no longer or perhaps have never served you. And with this grounding you will literally have the physical ability needed to *walk* away or make a course correction.

In closing today's teaching, feel your feet always under you, supporting your physical vehicle as your soul leads the way.

And So It Is.

# Teaching 9:
# Remain a Humble Servant

"Do you desire to construct a
vast and lofty fabric?
Think first about the foundations of humility.
The higher your structure is to be,
the deeper must be its foundation."

**Saint Augustine**

EVERY SOUL that is truly enlightened knows to always remain a humble servant. There are several components to humble servitude. Both humility and service reside within every enlightened being and for anyone's work to inspire; the two must be always combined. Through the act of service to others, one will deepen their knowledge of themselves. Trade your ego for humility. This will benefit not only the servant, but also those who are being served. For remaining in your humbleness as a servant to those around you will light the way for the path of all others who are ready for their own illumination.

We wish to share some suggestions on how to serve others. From time to time, in your good opinion you may find someone who could benefit from your unique service. First and most importantly, never assume that you have the permission to be of service to another without their explicit consent. It is the most respectful practice to wait for an invitation from those who desire your services.

If you are in the service of healing, never assume that those who may in fact benefit from a service that you offer actually have the desire to be healed. Not all of those who are in fact ill intend to be well. And for those who do find wellness, do not assume you are the reason another gets well. Although you may take credit for your willingness and ability to transport the gift of wellness into physical form, true healing only occurs in the perfect time, in the perfect form through the intention of those who receive it.

Let us also offer ways to take care of yourself. During any mutually agreed healing experience, do not go blindly bumping into the energy of those who receive your gifts. Protect your own system before entering their energy field. Also, do not enter into your service work alone. Ask for help from your spiritual support team during the time it takes to facilitate your work.

No matter how you are called to serve others, service combined with the feelings of gratitude and grace will also allow you to remain in your humility. Embracing these feelings will allow you to deeply express yourself and the gifts you have each come to earth to share with others. Great works can only be accomplished by those with a heart full of grace and thankfulness. And a graceful heart will always reach the hearts of those who are ready to remember their own divinity.

A fundamental characteristic of a humble servant is to remain in a state of awe by acknowledging the unique gifts of all other divine beings you meet on your journey. For just as your path was illuminated in front of you, so shall theirs be. And practice residing in reverence of your journey's beginnings. Keep this memory and story alive while serving others, for without it you may have not begun. Always be thankful to the helpers who supported and believed in you. These are the earthly angels who shined their lights so that you were able to see. It will require the strength of the collective marching forth to forge a new path for all of humanity now. And So It Is

# Teaching 10:
# Accept Abundance

"You pray in your distress and in your need;
would that you might also pray
in the fullness of your joy and in
your days of abundance."

**Khalil Gibran**

AAH THE grace and the glory that abounds our universe and surrounds our hearts. If you only knew the endless source of abundance, you would never fear again of having not enough. To begin, there is no such thing as *not enough*. It is an impossibility in this universe. The universal mind does not have a place to house that thought. Enough and plenty are available to all. The only question when speaking on abundance is who shall choose to tap the Source?

Who shall tap the source of the flow of abundance and allow it to come forth into their lives like rivers flowing from waterfalls? The waterfall believes in the water, therefore co-creating an endless flow. In fact, it never sees itself as separate from the water at all.

The heavens also want you to be in abundance, for abundance is the way and the path to your heavenly duties on Earth. Tap into the Source and your path will be lit clearly for you at once. Not later today, not tomorrow, not some time in the distance of your future. At once! Source tapping will release your doubt and allow you to fulfill your life's work. And like the infinite nature and law of abundance, there is an infinite amount of work to be done on Earth. This time of now is a critical moment, a critical phase of Mother Earth's development. We must have many who are in the flow of abundance for the work needs to be done now.

All of you must believe in your soul's power to create. Believe that you can each make a great difference. Abundance is there for you, just as much as it is for your neighbors. We do not say you may have some but another gets more. It is your choice and always up to you. It is not for us to decide. Free choice and free will demands that. It is true for all things including the nature and law of abundant living. Your life is meant to be rich and full of fruit, unless *you* chose for it not to be.

In human form you block the flow first with your belief about yourselves and who you are, where you came from, how much you are worth, and what you deserve. These beliefs are small in many of you, meaning you believe that you are small. This is untrue, and pretending to be small will not serve you. Insignificance is one of the most disrespectful beliefs you have about yourselves. It is not who you are.

The next human block to abundance is in your mind. Some of your thoughts may be "I don't deserve this, I can't make this happen. Who am I to take so much? If I had all of what I need what would I do with it? The responsibility is too large. I will be better to just stay with what I have now, it's what I know." One's relationship to abundance is in direct synchronicity with their relationship to themselves. If they attract little, they think little of themselves. Some of you call this humility, or being humble. Thoughts of deprivation are not humble. Deprived thoughts are not natural and were never your soul's intention.

Deprivation is different from a life of simplicity. Simplicity is good, it allows for focus and clarity in your heart and mind. Clutter can at times block the flow from an environmental sense. But abundance with right purpose and intent is always good. True abundance knows there is plenty for all, for me and for others, and sharing this abundance is good.

One moment on sharing your abundance with others. Many do not know this. Share the abundance and allow it to flow from your heart with others. But only share your abundance when you have truly disengaged the ego from expectation of its return to you. Give and let go. Truly let go. And another point on this: remain humble about your gift and your generosity. When ego is involved in the gift giving it is not a gift. If your intention is not pure it will often cause a disconnection between yourself and the receiver, because it was done from ego, not from an abundant heart.

Jesus and the story of the fish and loaves is an example of sharing with a pure abundant heart. Many came to experience Him and hear what He knew, and had to share with others, hence the amount of fish and loaves. He did not do this just once, as you can imagine. It was often. And there was plenty. The manifestation of the fish and loaves was also a teaching on abundance. Jesus would say, "If I can create this abundance for all who are here with me now, so is the same for you. The only difference between us is your limited belief in your ability to create." Abundance is available to all. You only need to believe in yourself first, and then in the abundance of the Infinite. In-finite. There is no such thing as finite, perhaps in your tables of mathematics, but not in Universal Creation.

It is easy to begin your relationship with abundant living. Spend time seeing the river of abundance flow through your "Crown" and into your heart with pureness of intention. Then plan for abundance to flow on your path. See it here in your life now, already occurring and feel the joy in your heart as you say yes to abundance. See yourself surrounded by abundance as the river flows through the doorways of your homes and flows into the lives of all that reside there. And as you are fully bathed in the river of abundance now, see your feet firmly planted and walking on purpose, carrying your vehicle while you are doing the deeds you came here to do. In this vision, see your hands reaching outward sharing it with every soul you are blessed to meet on your divine path.

And So It Is.

# Teaching 11:
# Tread Lightly on Mother Earth

"For in the true nature of things,
if we rightly consider,
every green tree is far more glorious than
if it were made of gold and silver."

**Martin Luther King**

WE GUIDE, share and impart this wisdom through you and to the people with great love and great joy, for it is time. Know this. It is time for the great change. The great transformation of this beautiful home on Mother Earth is now. Many have been walking asleep on her paths. It is time to wake them.

Mother Earth is in need of regeneration, in need of care, in need of cleansing. She is deeply saddened by the damage and the toil the people of now have taken on her. There has been great disrespect and this has saddened her deeply to her core. She knows that many of you don't know any better way. But for those who do, it is time to wake those who walk with heavy feet on her sacred ground. These ones think they own her, and this is not so. You are all residing in her home as a guest, not She in yours.

The great animals walking on her soil know this wisdom and continue to try to do their part, their jobs that they have come naturally to do. But they have very little help, very little support from the two legged ones, and are feeling injured by this damage and brutality against them with the lack of respect or awareness on the part of the two-legged's. They are dying in numbers the Earth has never recorded before and are unable to regenerate in the ways they used to, the ways that nature intended. The two-legged's are unwilling as a whole, to share the space and are hungry with greed. The greed of the two-legged's is doing damage too rapidly to allow regeneration of the beautiful creatures of the planet. You will soon know the irony of this story's outcome. You will know that it is *you* that cannot exist without *them*. And killing them off is actually the act of killing yourselves. Our language is strong here. It is intended to be because you must pay attention.

People before you knew how to respect Mother Earth and her great creatures. All creatures great and small are great creatures, all with a job and a purpose serving themselves, and serving the two- legged's and serving to balance and maintain the harmony of their great Mother. What they reap, they also naturally sow by practicing the necessity of giving back. Planting, germinating, and regenerating is the natural wisdom and practice of the creatures.

You have forgotten your natural rhythms and abandoned your knowing of the natural cycle of all creatures and of the Earth, and you have torn holes in her very fabric. These holes are not regenerating. This damage that has occurred with great violence and speed has natural consequences. What has been raped in only a century's time cannot be restored to health and balance. This planet will always be scarred from this time on her journey. You have left a scar, and She will heal this would with or without you.

Be certain of this: She wants you here. She welcomes you. But you must return to her as helpers only. Help her repair this wound you have inflicted. And help her creatures re-nourish themselves. You have been wasting their flesh, drying up their water sources, and turning their grass to concrete. Tread lightly upon her sacred ground and be thankful for the sustenance and warmth she provides. She wants you here, but she does not need you. You do not own her.

Return to ways of respect. This relationship is toxic for her now and this is a great sadness. You have betrayed her and taken advantage of her kindness, generosity, and her gifts. She can live without you, and she will replenish herself and live on. You cannot live, at least here on this planet, in this way, in these bodies, having these unique experiences without her. If you want to continue your relationship, you need to make your amends and return to the ways you once remembered and become helpers in her recovery. Recover Earth. Re-Cover Earth.

Practice a more natural way of being by observing the practices of nature. Some of you, although very few still, already know. Watch them. Join with them. Learn from those among you that already know how. You must be speedy in this tutorship. And each of you that join must wake up three more to also join in the re-covering. There is much to do in the way of recovery. Participate in a task to re-cover Mother Earth and ignite a passion for it. Contribute also in the recovery of the creatures that roam the Earth. Partake daily in these tasks while waking three more helpers and go about this work ahead of you. If this is done quickly, you will be able to stay, the relationship will go on.

Many of you have the mind that if you join in the recovery, you will have to give something up that you have attached to that creates comfort in your lives. Your thinking mind is incorrect with this belief. If you do not become helpers and complete this task, you will lose more than your comforts. You will lose everything.

The creatures that remain on Earth, the one's you have not yet eliminated, can also be helpers. First stop the needless elimination and waste of their flesh. Second, observe their ways and their nature. You can learn much from their natural way to teach you how to balance your own. Ask yourselves in your observation of them: What do they need? How much do they take? How do they commune? In what ways and forms do they gather together? How do they replenish? How do they heal? Whom do they listen to? Where do they naturally grow and flourish? How do they birth? How do they cooperate? How do they give back? This final question is the most important for you to learn now. Start there. And proceed forth. The first task is to Re-cover Mother Earth Now.

And So It Is.

# Teaching 12:
# Reveal Thy Self

"Glorify who you are today,
do not condemn who you were yesterday,
and dream of who you can be tomorrow."

**Neale Donald Walsch**

IN ORDER to know thy self, you must do your own healing. This is particularly true when you will be working with healing energies of others. You can only take others as far as you have travelled yourself. Lack of deeper examination of the Self will only allow for surface results when you are working with others. Do your work. Know your human wounds. Know the places within that need healing. This is needed for one to become a master of their soul.

Are your wounds in your past? Who are those that you have not forgiven? Begin by forgiving yourself and then you will move into the forgiveness of others who have injured you. In fact bless them and thank them for loving you enough to incarnate as one of your teachers in this lifetime. It is often those who have caused the most injury to your current lives that are your greatest teachers disguised as your enemies. Release and let go of the "past" for there is no time *than* the present.

How shall you let go of the past? Remember the truth of the spiral. It is all happening all the time. Time does not flow in a straight line. Time is happening now in all the ways and with all the experiences you have had, are having and ever will have. Time folds in on itself and continues to return to us, just at different levels of remembering. This is why the lessons that are repeated time and again return to you. Time is a spiral, not a straight line. Use this remembrance and truth about time when you are healing yourselves. Your history is as present as the amount of time you spend thinking about it. Release the old stories and beliefs of your life that no longer serve you. Then move into a level of vibration that will expedite your recovery so you can become a more efficient and a clear vessel for the healing of others.

Examine yourself at a deeper level. Become willing to reveal your unedited truths. These truths will reveal yourself back to yourself showing you the places within that require more healing. These may be blocks or fears, or historical memories that could block the clarity and communication of your vessel. The time that you take to do this healing work is important time. If you do not heal yourself you cannot authentically offer your Divinity to another. If you do continue on your own path of growth and development you can have the nurturing relationships you all deserve to experience.

Use tools of healing that resonate with your own body, mind and soul. When you are healing your wounds with the tools of your choice, also remember this truth: Love is the vibration needed for healing. Each one of you comes from love, are love incarnate in the time of now, and will flow back to love when you return home.

And So It Is.

# Teaching 13:
# Enter Into Sacred Relationships

**"Everything that irritates us about another can lead us to an understanding of ourselves."**

**Carl Jung**

WE BEGIN this teaching on sacred relationships by reminding you to always nurture the relationship with yourself first. I know we have been saying this often, and it is important to remember this always. It is the cornerstone of all relationships you enter into, with the Divine, with your beloved, with friends, working relationships, and with all the creatures of this Earth.

Begin nurturing your relationship with yourself by speaking kind words to yourself. Using a harsh tone damages the cells of your body and muddies your waters internally. This truth is becoming known to some of you now. Your words are power. They injure and they nurture. Remember this. They are one of your greatest tools. Use them wisely. Practice words of love with self often until this practice becomes natural for you. Send yourself kind words and once you begin to believe them, these words of kindness will flow more readily to others with whom you speak.

More on relationships and how to treat them as sacred, as they were meant to be: Be watchful of whom you are attracted to, and not just in a sexual way, although that also matters. Who do you choose to *spend* your time with? Those whom you seek out are there to mirror who you are at that point of time in your life. You are always changing and so those you are attracted to vibrationally will also change. This is why the current expectation of the length of marital relationships does not always work out the way they were initially intended. Your own vibrations are ever changing and the relationship with yourself also changes.

Attaching to another permanently for a lifetime may feel somewhat restricting once you change enough from the point of the initial attraction. All relationships ebb and flow and allowing for adjustments will serve your natural growth experience. Tethering yourselves to anyone for longer than the relationship serves purpose will slow down your vibration, thereby slowing the growth of your soul. It also does not serve the other whom you may be tethered, even though they may resist the release.

As mentioned, relationships must be in service to both people for that time. It was never intended that you *must* remain with only one for all time. This practice, although nurturing to some, may not serve all. There are only a small number involved in those contracts that walk amongst you now. And as your world is speeding up its vibrational energy force, and you are realizing that time is clearly non-linear (you are all feeling this,) relationships are also speeding up. Contracts with one another are taking less time and therefore you are seeing relationships come to a close in larger numbers than before.

More of you are remembering that you are divine souls and you are coming closer to God and what that means for you. And the closer you get to this truth, the less desire you will feel to build in superficial intensity within your relationships. To allow yourselves to blend harmoniously with your authentic nature, shower all of your relationships with free choice at all times. Be free and you will be equals, for freedom is a cornerstone for sacred relationship.

By nature you each have free choice and requiring anyone to be bound in relationship is not in service, is not of God, and did not come from God, as you have been previously taught. This idea came from man, and was born out of fear and birthed into the world during a time when conformity was developing. Man formed these rules and requirements and then called them in the name of God so they would be followed.

Now you are collectively living in a time where some of you are waking up to whom you truly are, and being bound in any form will no longer serve you. Being bound will no longer serve any true purpose; it will in fact restrict you. It will restrict your size, your speed, your voice, your knowing, and your human journey. You are greater than the binds that tether you. Release them if that serves you more, if that serves you kindly, and creates freedom for you.

Let us speak more broadly now of the binds or ties to any institution that you find yourself in that feels restricted. There are too many contracts on the planet at this time in business, in life, in relationships, and in homes. Many of them are blocking the natural flow and natural order of your souls. These contracts are now being broken everywhere. You are seeing this in contracts with your homes, your institutions, jobs, marriages, with your monies, in your banks and many other systems. It is the contracts that restrict your freedom that are no longer serving you as a whole. This contractual system is hierarchical and you are not. You are all part of the Divine One and these hierarchies will eventually come down.

Release as many contracts as those that no longer serve you as a people. Contracts that bind you to the same path, to the same mind, to the same energies, to the same individuals, to the same communities were not created by Source and are all based in fear. Freedom will bring equality in all relationships, for then you have choice and you will no longer have to fear that something will be taken from you. This will free you to enter only into relationships that walk in love, that connect in love and allow for freedom.

Allow yourselves to change your minds about how you enter all relationships and this one thing will change your collective path. It is required for individual and collective growth. Base all of your relationships only in love and at all times allowing all those who enter to be showered with the freedom of choice. Redefine your relationships. This one change will change your world.

And So It Is.

# Teaching 14:
# Connect to Source

**"There comes a time when the mind takes a higher plane of knowledge but can never prove how it got there."**

**Albert Einstein**

REMEMBER THAT we are always connected to all that ever was, is now, and ever shall be. We are always connected. And spending time to get in touch with that connection is important. Whenever you deliberately take the time to connect through your human rituals you strengthen your connection to us and with your own divine soul. There is no need to rush. Take the time through your intention and prayer to establish a clear conscious connection.

One of the benefits of consciously connecting is that it allows you to connect with your body. Always come into your body and connect from there. Do not detach or attempt to connect from another place outside your body. That would result in a less clear connection and is not suggested. You need your body as the tool, the vehicle of connection. It is there to serve you. Do not disregard this when you are connecting to Source and tuning into the Divine frequency.

Come into your body first with ease, not haste. Visualize your core and connect your core with the core of Mother Earth and up into the heavenly realm and call in those from the heavens that come from Source that love you. These are beings that know your heart, and your way, and your path and are willing to assist you on your way.

We offer the following visualization for establishing a clear and conscious connection to Source:

Always start by coming into your body. Call yourself into your body to use it as the vehicle for connection. Once inside your vehicle, begin by gently connecting with your breath. With each inhale breathe in love for self, allowing that love to settle into your heart space. Then allow the breath of life to travel down further into your core. You can find your core in the belly area and illuminate the light of your own core with the breath of life.

Once you have illuminated your own power, then visualize the crystallized channel from your inner core moving down, through your body into your seat and then down into the crust of Mother Earth. Allow your channel to continue travelling down through the layers of Mother Earth, through her ocean floor and down into Her core.

See the core of Mother Earth illuminated and waiting to connect with your channel. Then as your channel meets with the core of Mother Earth, wrap the light of your channel around the loving core of Mother Earth. Thank Mother Earth for accepting your connection and giving you the ability to stabilize your body and feel the balance of your feet on the ground while connecting to her ancient wisdom.

Now that you are connected to Mother Earth's core, return your focus to the core within your own body. Now begin to expand and stretch your crystalline channel upwards through your heart. See it illuminate and open your heart and as it moves into your throat your channel also illuminates your voice. See it now passing behind your mind's eye to illuminate your third eye and then up through your crown as it opens to the heavens. Send your crystal channel up now into the sky, through your galaxy and into the cosmos and reaching the heavens where it begins to swirl and spiral. You can now see and greet your guides and helpers from heavenly Source.

See all the beings that know you and love you-ancestors, angels, ascended masters, and beings you once knew that passed over in this lifetime to help in your continued journey on Earth. Ask them to gather and join around you. See them all forming in a circle of grace around your connection.

Thank them for joining you today in your connection and ask them to assist you in connecting to the heavenly wisdom that is available for you on this day. And if there is a Source being you wish to call forth specifically to speak with you through this channel you have now created call them forth now and ask that their presence join yours.

Once you have done so, you may now return to the illuminated core within yourself. And finally, with an open heart, tune into the frequency of those you called forth and begin to listen to the voice of the Divine.

And So It Is.

# Teaching 15:
# Know You Are the Miracle

**"Do this in memory of me."**

**Jesus**

THIS IS a day of celebration and rebirth, for Easter represents a day of great light. The love that is felt today on parts of this planet comes from the memory of the path of Jesus Christ and how He gave this miracle of light to the people years ago.

This miracle of life is about how He in His form manifested the miracle of life. It was in order for the people to remember who they really are and that they too possessed what He had, if only they would awaken it within themselves. They could also bring great light forth, bringing miracles to themselves and one another. He gave the gift of rebirth and the miracle of life and this day is a representation of that memory. There is a memory you all hold in your own cellular memory and Mother Earth holds in her records, and that we in the heavens know; that there is life after life after life after life.

We in the heavens are life embodied in spirit from. Those of you on the Earth now are spirits embodied in human form. It is your job now on the planet to remember the miracle of life and rebirth. If you live in the celebration of this memory every day you will know pure joy. You will never fear again, because you will know, as your soul knows, that each one of you is indeed a miracle.

Jesus demonstrated this for you. The miracles of Jesus did not happen in the ways it was later written. There was interference in the true teaching and the message that would eventually be sent forth. You have been told by man that this miracle that was performed by my Beloved, was performed in order to remove the sins of the people, and that He gave his life to purify the sins of man. This is not so and could never be so, since there is no true thing as a sin. Humans are not sinners in the way that you define them to be.

Jesus's true purpose was to display the action of rebirth and the miracle of returning to life in physical form to show how miraculous every human truly is in physical form. This was done so that humans could shed their old thought forms about themselves that are not in service of who they really are. Jesus wanted every Spirit in human form to know they have the ability to shed those lower vibrations and transform that energy into Source energy that creates the miracle of life itself. Man took this and bent the message by calling these lower vibrations sins against God. Man then created entire religions based on this false interpretation.

But now you are slowly waking up and remembering the truth of your soul. And I am here to remind you of that truth. You all possess the memory that you are all the miracles that the planet needs in this time. You can each use your power within to perform them now. Jesus knew this and showed you the way. You too must rise to the knowing of this truth.

It is a new day, a new dawn and a new energy is coming to your planet. More and more of you are waking up to this new day, new life, new breath, new knowing of what your soul has truly always known. Until now, you have just been walking in sleep, deciding to not remember your greatness and your true light and abilities. You all have the ability to not only miraculously heal yourselves, but all on the planet. And some of you are now coming together in greater numbers to remember this, and do this work. That is why you are here at this time incarnate: to remember the true path, the true way, the true light that Jesus embodied years ago.

Return to His wisdom, return to His knowledge, return to His records, his *true* records. All you have to do is sit quietly and ask Him, and you will know. Just call on Him and His remembrance and what he experienced and showed the people at that time and he will show each of you the way, to the powerful light that resides within each of you. He can assist in illuminating your divine light if you so choose.

The real story of His time on the planet was recorded falsely by man. This did not happen by accident. In fact it was meant to be, as all that comes forth is meant to be. His deeds and His message were in fact meant to be misinterpreted. He knew that this was part of a much larger purpose. One of His gifts to those who would hear of his "story" later was the gift of misinformation. Without knowing through embodied experience what you are not, you cannot truly find your own way to truly embracing who you are.

It took a long time on the planet to walk in sleep before the reawakening, but it is coming to you now. You were meant to walk in sleep and be fed the story of who you are not in order to make a choice for yourselves that this false message is not your truth. This false message force fed to you and reinforced by many men was a gift so that you who chose to not fully digest it could have the free will to choose again. And in this choosing, you can decide and define and declare who you really are, and what your true story is without the interference of another telling you who you should be and what you should believe. This was a gift from Christ.

Jesus continues to have many miracles to show you all. And you need true miracles now, for much healing is required. Jesus knows this and has healed many. His power was so great that it has lived on for more than two millennia and He is still very much with you.

I say to you all, do not wait for the dawn to arrive. Make it happen. Stand in the grand vision of the great knowing. Do not sit and wait. Create the dawn. Those who choose to remain idle are not true servants. We need all of you to stand and create a healing on this planet and with one another. Gather your resources; know your plan and set forth to create your new beginning.

Light is also required for the new beginning. A new energy infused with light is needed for the healing to occur. Darkness shrouds your lands as a heavy burden now that each of you feels in your hearts. The darkness is old energy and much of it is ready to be shed. Cast the darkness away and welcome in the light. Call on help from the sun to come in all of its glory to infuse and energize the planet with this new vibration.

Let it not be only Easter that you call a day of rebirth. It is not meant for only one day of each calendar year. Rebirth must be celebrated each day. You think and celebrate in ways that are much smaller than you know.

With pure joy and harmony know that your souls are one with Source. You are a divine creator and every moment the power of miracles lie at the tips of your fingers. Take the energy and infuse it into your daily practices. Become ready for your illumination by calling in the energy of rebirth consciously and you will be ready for manifestation.

You can have this great awakening every day. Call in Jesus to assist with this infusion of miraculous Source energy. You are all able to be a part of and manifest miraculous Source energy. It is not bigger than you; it is not only for Jesus the Divine manifestor. You are the divine!

The miracle of rebirth is not only for those you define as gurus or enlightened ones. You all possess the ability to enlighten in this very moment. You all have that power. All you have to do is know that you are the path, you are the knowledge, the wisdom, the source, the miracle. Take it into your hands, with the memory that you and Jesus are One. This is what He showed you with His rebirth. Remember that. Believe that. Manifest that. Be that. You cannot truly separate from Source. Most of you just walk on this human path without memory. Remember, and it is yours.

For your summary: Your earthly task is to walk in the power of your light and share it with all you meet so they will remember the light within themselves. Your heavenly task is to remember that you are One with the Divine in every breath, and that you are all miraculous origins of Source. Go forth to perform miracles for yourselves and with those that are ready for rebirth. And stand in awe of those who are also rebirthing themselves and sharing their miracles with more and more. And so it goes on and on and on.

We offer the following statement to practice this teaching aloud whenever you wish to consciously invoke your own miraculous Source energy:

### Invoking the Miracle

I thank this new day for illuminating my heart now.

I bask in the glory of the divine light within.

I call in the dawn and return to my Self.

I choose to begin again and again.

I am born anew on this day,

for I am the miracle.

And So It Is.

# Teaching 16:
# Be Thankful

"If the only prayer you ever say in your
entire life is thank you, it will be enough."

**Meister Eckhart**

BE THANKFUL for everything. Take time to see the beauty within all of your blessings and all of your consequences. It is all perfect. It is there for you, teaching you, loving you, and reminding you. Be thankful for all of your circumstances, blessing, relationships, graces, miracles, and hardships.

As a divine being in human form call in grace, call in glory, and spend your time in joy. Joy will call in more joy, grace will call in more grace, love will call in more love, and gratitude will call in more gratefulness.

Think grateful thoughts. Thank your blessings by speaking of them often with your voice. State with your words how blessed you are. Your words of gratitude are powerful. Spend time sharing your gratefulness with others. Be thankful in your prayers. Bring gratitude into your body and allow it to rest in your heart. That is where it lives. And a thankful heart is the heart of an enlightened soul.

You all deserve good. The more you notice the goodness around you that comes into your life in every way and every circumstance, the more will come. This is the way of gratitude. It is the natural law of like attracts like. It is not a law of opposites. There are laws of opposites in your universe, but this is not one of them. When you are in a state of awe, a state of pure thankfulness for what you have brought forth, what you have received from others, and what you have been gifted from the Divine, then abundance must flow.

We mentioned this flow of abundance in an earlier teaching. See it flowing like a river into your home, into your hearts, and flowing around all those who reside in your home. See it then pouring forth into the homes of all others who choose to open their doors and accept abundance in.

Be grateful and give thanks for more than your blessings. Thank your consequences. Thank the circumstances and the people in your life that you may perceive as blocks or difficulties. The people you relate to in your life in a difficult way love you enough to create a human experience of disconnection. They are the Great Reminders in human form. Those that walk amongst you that you wish would not have crossed your path, do not shun them. They are there crossing your path at the exact moment you need a reminder of who you are and what you are doing here. They are urging you to reconnect to your soul's knowing so that you can be thankful for all of it. There are no mistaken circumstances or people in your life that should not be there. There are no chance meetings. It was all pre-arranged and every one of them is a gift for you.

These pre-arrangements with the Great Reminders always include free will once the divine meeting is activated. Although your soul has called it forth, it is always your choice what you wish to do with these opportunities in human form. What kind of experience will you choose? Do you wish to shun your difficult relationships and choose to feel betrayed and victimized? Will you choose anger and work your way toward resentment? It is a short journey, from anger to resentment, but not one that is recommended or necessary.

Another choice is to see the beauty in any human difficulty. You have the ability to choose thankfulness for the difficulties and to only respond with love. See these difficulties as an opportunity for yourself to show up in your true form. When a difficulty arises, it offers an opportunity for you to decide, "Who do I choose to be now?" You can choose a grateful heart and transform these lower vibrations of the ego into thankfulness, but it is always your choice. We will never interfere in your experiences of deciding who you are in every moment.

In closing this teaching, we offer that you remember this: While traveling your human journey, thankfulness is the way to enlightening your soul.

And So It Is.

# Teaching 17:
# Call on Your Support Team

**"Only from the alliance of the one,
working with and through the other,
are great things born."**

**Antoine de Saint-Exupery**

MASTERY OF the human self requires support. Know that you do not travel this journey alone. You have many helpers, helpers from Mother Earth and also throughout the heavens. Use both support teams from your physical realm and the heavenly realm as you travel your human path. Your helpers are here to co-create the blessings and the abundance in your life. You can call on these helpers at any time to come and assist you. Use them with the intention of love that comes from a pure heart. Ask them to assist you on your path and be grateful for the help.

Remember that you are never truly alone and you have much help. Your ego would have you believe that this human journey can be done alone. It cannot, and when you try, you will be blocked. Your ego may announce, "I will do it alone and I will take full credit..." It is untrue. Whenever you say, "I can do this alone" you are choosing to attempt to disconnect from Source. Whatever you are determined to do alone, you will not truly complete, or it will take an awfully long time on an arduous path to completion.

Calling on your support team for guidance will expedite whatever it is you wish to create. The experience of co-creation will allow it to manifest with greater ease, speed, clarity, lightness and purity of form. The process of co-creation will allow you manifest great work. The river of creation will flow when you connect to Source by asking for assistance.

Assistance is around you and available at all times and it can come in instantly. All we need from you is to be invited, for we never interfere. We will come and be with you to co-create an experience, a message, a masterpiece, or a life form. We are always here for you and it is our joy to assist in the process.

In addition to your heavenly helpers, human support in physical form is also available to you. You will meet them when your paths cross at the exact time that the opportunity presents itself for co-creation. And again, it is your choice to plug in and make the connection with your physical support.

You may meet another that crosses your path that you were not expecting to show up. See this unforeseen meeting as an opportunity and if it feels good to you, accept it as an invitation to co-create with these physical helpers. Be aware of these meetings by asking self: "Why have I met this person now, and what is the opportunity that is being presented in front of me with this person that has crossed my path?"

Choose your physical support wisely. You may wish to pause for council from your helpers in the heavens before accepting physical support. Some of you will ask for more physical support than others by gathering larger circles and some will gather only a few. The support team will ebb and flow on your journey depending on what you are creating at that time.

Both your physical and heavenly support teams will change as you progress on your journey. That is good. Blending a variety of energies throughout different experiences and purposes is beneficial. If you choose to remain static within a single support system, that is your choice. However, it often does not allow for the natural flow that is required to continue co-creating from fresh perspectives with new growth.

There are gifts and experiences that are unique to each of your support members. You may have the desire for different energies and wisdom depending on your intention and your place on the path. Very few of you have only one creation to bring forth into the light. A variety of creations will bring opportunity for a unique range of support.

When choosing your support team from the heavenly helpers and those of the earth to assist you on your divine path, be sure that the support serves the purpose, needs, intentions and desires for all involved. Use your help wisely and be in reverence of all the help that each of you have available to you at all times. And when the support you have called in feels complete or no longer serves purpose on your path, send a blessing, be thankful, and release.

And So It Is.

# Teaching 18:
# Trust the Source

"The mind, once expanded to the dimensions
of larger ideas,
never returns to its original size."

**Oliver Wendell Holmes**

YOUR HUMAN path will be traveled with greater ease if you take trust along for the journey. We offer two ways to practice trusting in Source. The first involves the direction your life path takes you, and the second is how to trust when Divine source is communicating with you on your travels.

First, realize that you did choose the life path you are on. Your human journey is, in fact, a divine assignment that your soul arranged and agreed to before incarnating in this lifetime. From your current vantage point it is understandable that some of you may have feelings about choosing the human journey that you are currently traveling. This is also natural. You may have thoughts such as, "I didn't ask for this. How could I have planned these circumstances? This is not how my life was supposed to turn out!"

We agree that some human circumstances and experiences are indeed challenging to endure. And even certain events send your life path in a completely unexpected direction, turning your physical life inside out. This "change" of plans will often create turmoil, requiring a rearrangement of your physical world and sometimes even some of the people in it. For those travelers who wish to remain asleep, the journey will be more difficult. Walking the path of your soul's true purpose will require upheaval of the status quo in your physical surroundings and circumstances.

Very often these experiences show up out of the blue. If this happens then know that it was set up that way. You were meant to be caught off of your *guard* because there is not a lot of planning to be done in human form. The human ego likes to plan and strategize, creating time tables and schedules. We in the heavenly realms don't need such things, and therefore when you make these contracts to do your divine work on Earth, you say, "Catch me off guard, for if I involve ego enough in my human form to plan something such as this I would muddle it up. My ego will interfere in the divine perfection of it all. If my ego is involved I may even miss the whole point."

You may at first perceive change as loss. We understand that on a human level the kind of reorganization that is necessary for soul advancement can be painful, even bringing up feelings of anger or resentment. If anger comes to you, we do not judge it. We know that the anger is part of the natural human process for many of you. There are very few who choose to go merrily along in a completely unexpected life direction. Some of you do, but most resist, feeling anger at some point along the way. When anger shows up do not make it worse by judging yourselves. Know that we understand and we love you. You can trust that Universal Source is both patient and unconditional.

An additional area where trust can be a concern is discernment while Source is communicating with you. Trust that we communicate with you all in a number of ways. You may sometimes doubt your own ability, willingness and worthiness to even have a connection with Source. Just notice that fear is present and your ego is attempting to block you from remembering your divinity. This does not change our relationship with you. This does not change our love for you. We understand that it is part of the human experience of learning how to trust. In time and with practice, you will learn to trust the divine voice that you are hearing and use the information to benefit your journey.

Some of you may even pause and say, "I am making this up, this cannot be real. This must only be my imagination." This is also human. Just notice that it comes from a place of your own shame and doubt as ego is attempting to foster separation and disbelief. This kind of interference is coming from your lower vibrational self where ego is housed because ego wants you to disconnect from the voice of Source. This is natural, for if you listen and take action in what you are being called to do, it may eventually put ego out of a job.

Confusion often arises when it becomes difficult to discern between the voice of the Divine, and your ego's voice. With practice you will learn how to decipher between the two. Do not fear. All who are in the process of becoming fully realized go through a similar experience. When it is difficult to discern where the message is coming from, take a glance at the information that you have gathered and ask yourself, "Does the message that is being communicated foster fear or faith? Does it bring me down or raise me up? Does it serve the material world or the spiritual? Does it restrict or expand my life? These answers will inform you if the messages you are receiving are coming from your ego or if you are truly in contact with the Source of your soul. This practice will enhance your ability to discern and trust so that you can go confidently in the direction of your soul's calling.

Some of you may make a conscious decision, even in the face of all that has happened in your awakening to disengage and return to a life that you knew before your awakening began. You always have the choice and freedom to go back to sleep. You may be on the fence asking yourself, "Should I return to the familiar life that I knew before or should I maintain my pace on this path and see what my soul has in store for me?" We would welcome you to make the latter choice. When deciding whether you should keep going, continue showing up for just one more day.

In closing for this teaching, regardless of where you are on your path of trusting your connection to Source, always remember this: Before your incarnation into this lifetime we made an agreement to co-create, at this exact time, for a divine purpose. And our relationship was meant to be.

And So It Is.

# Teaching 19:
# Let your Feelings
# Inform Your Path

**"Love is what we were born with.
Fear is what we learned here."**

**Marianne Williamson**

YOUR HUMAN feelings are the Great Informers for the journey of your soul. Get to know your feelings and what each of them represents and how they are informing you on your divine path. In order to do this, identify the feeling first. Each of your feelings, once you get to know them and what they represent for you and your journey, will inform you as to what kinds of experiences you are having in human form. And fear is the greatest informer of all of your feelings.

When you feel fear it is a much lower, dimmer vibrational energy than love, so much so that it is on the opposite end of the spectrum. This is so because fear does not come from Source. In fact if you are in fear it will inform you that you have moved away from your Source. You may then ask the question, "Well then, if I come from Divine Source, then why be given the option of feeling fear at all? Why not just remain in a constant state of love, if that is truly all Source is?"

We offer this: Fear was given as a human experience for two reasons. The first reason being, in your human form, fear instinctively informs you that you are in some kind of danger. It was given to you as a tool for your physical survival so that you may remain on the task of having your human experience. The second reason fear is a necessary part of humanity is that it is quite the opposite of love. And if you did not have the experience of fear you would not appreciate the full experience of love, or be able to identify when you are in love because that is all you would be and have nothing for your comparison. So fear's second job is to inform you where you are in relation to your Source, in other words how close you are to God. Fear is your compass.

The energy of love vibrates at the highest brightest frequency. When you are in love's presence, whether feeling your own love, or if you are in close proximity to love outside of yourself, this frequency will resonate within and actually raise your physical vibration. Yes, just being in the presence of love is all that is required to do so, for love is literally contagious.

Love is the only frequency we reside in in the heavenly realm. It is the constant experience amongst those of us who have returned to Spirit. In your human experiences, in addition to love, fear is required as the additional part of the package for the two reasons that we mentioned. There really are only two feelings. You give these two feelings many labels in your human forms on earth in order to further identify where you are in relation to your connection to Source. This is good, but when you are in confusion with so many labels, simplify and ask yourself one question: "Am I in love in this moment or am I in fear?" And if the answer is fear, ask yourself one further question: "Why have I chosen fear and how can I return to love?"

If in the moment you cannot identify your feeling, whether it be fear or love, (some of you have made a practice of detaching from feeling much at all,) then go to the words you are speaking and the thoughts you are thinking in your mind. These will give you further information necessary to identify fear or love. And then return to that second question if your answer is fear.

It is interesting to us how many of you choose fear so often. If this is true for you, there is a different question to be asked: "Why is choosing fear so important to me in this moment that I am willing to abandon who I really am, which is divine love?" Because when you are in a continuous state of fear you cannot be in love. And when you are in an ongoing state of living most of your life from a place of fear, you truly have abandoned love. And if you find the answer to what is so important to you that you are willing to abandon love, you will always find the response you are having comes from your human ego, the place that houses fear.

Fear is housed in ego, and ego is the home of disconnection. As we mentioned in a previous teaching, ego was born with the intention to disconnect from self and others. Its purpose is to move you away from, disrupt and detach you from Source. On the other side of this, love is housed in your heart, the home of connection. And the heart's intention is to connect you to yourself and others. The purpose of love is to move you closer to your Source, with the goal of reminding you that you are the Divine incarnate.

When you meet any being on your path and initially feel fear, choose to send it love instead. Always return love, even when met with aggression. Do not meet with aggression and match it with the same vibrational exchange. Notice the aggression. Notice the fear. And return only love. Love is the magic potion that dissolves fear and makes room for a miracle.

Now you can understand the human experiences of feeling love and fear are both necessary. They are each a compass that will show you at all times where you are in relation to Source so that you have the ability to find your way home.

And So It Is.

# Teaching 20:
# Become Watchful for
# Earthly Signals

**"For things to reveal themselves to us,
we need to be ready to abandon
our views about them."**

**Tich Nhat Hanh**

BE WATCHFUL for your earthly signals, for they are the Great Confirmers. They will serve as your confirmation of whether you are on your path and connecting to Source while performing your earthly tasks. Your earthly signals act like the stars above as the compass that guides your soul. Signals come in all forms and you may be surprised by when and where they show up in your life. They can show up in a variety of places and it is important to pay attention when they are attempting to reach you.

Your feelings are one of the earthly signals that confirm where you are on your path. Listen to them. The creatures that cross your paths are also signals confirming if you are on track. Thank them. Dreams are also a way for Spirit to send you messages. Record them. Music and lyrics that linger are there for a reason. Remember them. Words spoken by another that make you take pause are not by chance. Notice them. The intuitive feeling inside your belly that you just cannot shake is suggesting you pay attention. Act on them. Chance meetings are frequently an offering of a new energy in your life, perhaps a helper. Welcome them.

We offer these examples above as a reminder to be ever watchful of your surroundings. These are earthly signals that are sent by your soul's knowing to light your way. Use the information for the purpose it was intended. The signals are not random happenstance, as many of you believe. They are confirmations that the Universe offers to indicate that you are indeed advancing your soul. And So It Is.

# Teaching 21:
# Accept the Winds of Change

"I can be changed by what happens to me,
but I refuse to be reduced by it."

**Maya Angelou**

ACCEPT AND expect the winds of change for they are among all of you on the planet now. You all know that great change is happening now as we speak with you today and more is to come. Change has been happening on this Earth for all time and is necessary for the creation of new birth, new life, new growth, and new paths to be forged. There are currently two winds blowing now on your planet: the winds are blowing through your individual lives and are also strengthening to gale force on a collective level. Bless them and know that the winds are the Great Catalysts alerting you to a new time in both your individual lives and life on Mother Earth.

The experience of connecting to divine wisdom, listening to Source and awakening to your true nature requires great change individually. This reorganizes the physical realities and ways of living. At times these shifts can also reorganize the people in your lives. New people may be coming into your lives in order to create the new experience that you need for that time. Expect the winds of change to transform the energies all around you, within your physical body vibrationally, within your mind, your heart, and within your core. These changes happen at a cellular level and are necessary for the shift to occur.

Changes in your personal environment are also being seen. Those things that clutter and distract may begin to feel less necessary or may even begin to disappear, even without your conscious decision for it to be so. This is good, although it may not feel good at the time. As we mentioned in an earlier teaching, you may experience these unexpected changes as loss. And you may resist.

You may stomp your feet on your path and say "No, I don't want this!"

We offer that you resist less, for the winds of change are around you and clearing the debris on your path for a purpose, and more specifically for your soul's purpose. Accepting that energy instead of standing in its way will assist you. An attitude of acceptance will get you where you are going at a speedier rate and with less to block your way. And although you have free choice in this, we suggest that you allow it to flow through you, your body, the people in your life, your surroundings, your home, and through all those you meet on your path. Breathe in the cool air of change and allow it to transform you in the ways that will only serve your divine tasks.

The winds of change are also blowing now at a collective level on Earth. On all of your paths, although some of you remain unaware, collective change is affecting all of the continents of Mother Earth. The purpose of this collective wind is to stir up the energies that require new breath and fresh perspective on your planet. Every people, creed, industry, institution, and every family on Earth at this moment in time is affected by this now.

And the winds of change are becoming stronger as you propel into this new experience. The winds are increasing in speed and force. Many are resisting and attempting to reach out and hang on to anything that is still tied down to the old ways of being out of fear of being tossed aside or swept away in the rapid currents. Plant your feet firmly as these changes come. But we also suggest allowing them to reshape your individual lives and your collective communities. Breathe in and do not resist. Acceptance is the key for these changes are required for growth and new ways of living. It is a new day.

You will feel the winds more strongly everywhere. And at times the winds will bring forth dust, and rain in order to prepare you for new life and a new way of being. Wind in its natural state will kick up the dust, blurring your vision and line of sight. This dust storm will be disorienting and is meant to be, for that is part of the process. But many will be caught off guard and surprised by the change. Your vision will eventually clear once the rains come.

The rains fall in order to clear the air and settle the dust. They come also to wash away the old outmoded ways of living. There are times like these, when the rains must come in floods, just as your tears flood down your face when you feel something particularly intense. The rains are a natural part of the process and serve to cleanse.

The rains will also bless the soil with much needed water and allow new life to have a place to germinate. At this point of change, you may individually and collectively gather your seeds for planting. Prepare the soil for your new life consciously choosing only fresh seeds that serve your new ways of being. Plant those seeds in the hydrated soils and then step back with faith in your hearts, for whatever is consciously planted will indeed germinate and grow.

In summary: Each one of you must plant your feet firmly for the shift that is now coming individually and collectively to Earth. Loosen your grip on those things that you may wish to hang too tightly on and breathe in the fresh new air. Through the dust of disorientation, and the cleansing rains, prepare for the changes with acceptance. The energies of both the heavens and the people of the planet need to come together for this transformation in time to occur.

And So It Is.

# Teaching 22:
# Gather the Tools for Your Trade

**"The expectations of life
depend upon diligence;
the mechanic that would perfect his work
must first sharpen his tools."**

**Confucius**

THERE ARE many tools and rituals that humans can utilize to enhance divine connection. These tools are known as the Great Assistants. They come into your life and offer their energy to you on the journey for a particular time and purpose. And your tools are here with you to support your connection with the Divine wisdom of the heavens as well as the ancient wisdom of Mother Earth. Use them wisely.

And So It Is.

# Teaching 23:
# Bless the Challenges

"Only by contending with challenges
that seem to be beyond your strength
to handle at the moment
you can grow more surely toward the stars."

Brian Tracy

LEARN TO bless your earthly challenges. This is part of remaining present in your connection as a divine being. Do not give your energy away to those who annoy or attempt to disrupt you on the path. Remain centered within yourself and on your purpose, even in the midst of all that goes along with your physical experience. You will often find an opportunity to disconnect and become distracted and this may continue to be one of your human challenges. The distractions, noise and static of your physical world will always be present; it is the human challenge of embodying a divine soul. Perhaps instead of condemning these challenges, in the future you may choose to be thankful them.

Bless your challenges for they are your opportunities embodied. Their gift is to offer you the chance to decide what part of you wants to show up when they present themselves. They are happening on an experiential level so that you can decide who you want to be in the moment you are faced with the challenge.

Many of you feel that you do not choose these challenges and would rather live in bliss in every moment if given the chance. Bliss is good. As we mentioned in an earlier teaching, embracing love as your true nature is the goal of what you are doing in human form and love is where you are headed when you return home. But, for now, you are souls choosing a human experience in this lifetime and the challenging periods are just as informative as the times when you experience joy and peace.

During times when you are challenged or even just distracted by another's presence, you have a choice. Will you choose to you give your energy to the distraction, or will you maintain your energy and remain connected to Source? That is the question.

Your human challenges are the Great Disruptors and present themselves in a variety of ways. They may come in the form of a relationship. Certain relationships you enter into are meant to disrupt you on purpose, These can include intimate relationships, the families you create, the friendships you have, work relationships, institutions you are a part of, and the communities in which you are involved. If you are being challenged by any of these relationships in particular, it is purposeful. Also know this: Those in human form that are your greatest challenges are those that you once recognized in spirit form as part of your soul group. Together you chose to form a challenging relationship during this lifetime out of your love for one another and a deep desire to evolve spiritually.

Relationships are wondrous proving grounds for spiritual evolvement. These souls agreed to enter into relationship with you, perhaps in the form of a partner, child, parent, sibling, coworker, boss, neighbor, friend, or foe. They were willing to sign up for this task with you for the sole purpose of showing you a part of yourself that you have not yet found peace of acceptance with. These challenging relationships are always in service of showing you to yourself. They are born out of love, although you may not recognize them as loving once these relational challenges are activated in human form. If you were to remember the agreement when the task was set up you would know that in Spirit form, they are some of your biggest fans.

Let us offer other examples humans choose to experience challenges. Another challenging distraction can be found within your human body. Depending on the level of the disruption that shows up in your physical body, you may be more than annoyed by it. You may in fact, curse it and you also may curse God for it. This part of the teaching may be difficult to embrace, but we must share the truth with you. Any illness is a blessing in disguise.

Illness in the physical body, whether it is a mild complaint or a more severe condition, is there as an alert that you are not in balance. This imbalance eventually forces your physical energy system to take on a toxic tone. These toxic resonate with illness and house themselves in some part of your physical body.

Toxic tones can come from a variety of sources. They can arrive through your thoughts. They can also arrive with greater strength through thoughts turned into words, and at even greater strength still when you combine your thoughts and words, and incorporate them into action. Over time, your thoughts words and deeds that are negatively charged will accumulate within your energy system and form a disruption inside your physical body. The longer negativity is left to accumulate, the more serious the condition becomes.

Toxic tones that form illness can also be grown from things found within your external environment. They can come from chemical toxins, polluted air, water, food and synthetic chemicals. If you ingest any of these at a rate that your body can no longer sustain its own rate of elimination, a toxic tone will form in the body.

The company that you keep can also be a breeding ground for eventual illness. The people that you surround yourself with relates directly to how healthy your body remains. The more time you spend in the presence of those who do not serve your best and highest good, the more opportunity for you to create a toxic tone within your body that will eventually create illness.

Please note that we stated an opportunity for *you* to create the toxic tone. Yes, it is always *your* choice to create a toxic tone and you do so by spending enough time with a toxic energy to pull it into your body which eventually forms an illness. This is not being done to you. It is formed by your own will, and even if your will is subconscious, it is always your choice. Therefore, your physical body is the second form that a challenge may arise. Again, these challenges are collectively your Great Disruptors and they are here as gifts of opportunity for you to decide how you want to be once they present themselves.

The third form a challenge can present itself regards your life path. Some of you are challenged in this area and are uncertain of your true path and place in this world. This is a great opportunity, although you generally see it as a tremendous setback. Some of you are stumbling in the darkness trying to grasp onto something that feels familiar in order to find your footing and begin walking your true path. Be certain that you are not alone. Many of you are having this experience and it can cause distress.

We suggest to those of you who are feeling challenged in finding your way to your purposeful path, to begin with self. The answers are not out there. The answers to the question, "What is my path and my purpose?" are not to be found anywhere outside of yourself. The answers are not housed in your parents, or your current occupation, or behind the desk of your current boss. The answers are also not housed in your children. Your children will need to find their own answers to this question. Do not look to them for the answer. We mention this because some of you are confused by that point. The answer is only housed inside of you. If you are currently asking, "What is my path and purpose in this lifetime?" Your purpose is found within.

Your purpose in life generally does not magically arrive on an arbitrarily chosen birthday. For some of you, you were literally born remembering what you came to accomplish in this lifetime, and you never forgot or waivered from your knowing. Others find that they arrive on their purpose well into their twilight years. This is not to be judged. The point is, you did. You have been able to feel the experience of being on your purposeful path for the time that you are incarnate now. This is always good. And then there are those of you who come into your purpose near the midpoint of your life. Of the three, this is the more common route of finding your way to your path and coming to be on purpose.

It often takes until the midpoint to quiet the external voices in your head long enough to ask yourself the question, "What is *my* path?" This is because by midlife many of you have either become weary enough from the emptiness of how you have been spending your time, or angry enough that you have been blindly following someone else's agenda for your own life. You will recognize that you have reached this place of either emptiness or anger when you find yourself saying, "I don't want to spend on more moment of my life doing *this!*"

It is here at the midpoint when you generally find the time to take a pause and re-evaluate how you choose to spend the time you have left. You may find this task challenging. When searching for your answer, we offer that you become truly willing to listen without doubt or bargaining. And when you have illuminated your own truth, take the risk to change your course. You may crawl, walk one step at a time, or even take a giant blind leap of faith onto your path of purpose. How you get there is not nearly as important as the fact that you do.

In summary: These three broad categories of your human challenges are being offered here as general descriptions. There are an infinite variety of details in between that can challenge each of your journeys. We offer that you embrace your unique challenges, remembering that they come into physical form as your divine blessings in disguise.

And So It Is.

# Teaching 24:
# Go Where You Are Called

**"It is never too late to be what
you might have been."**

**George Elliot**

WE DEFINE the title of this teaching *Go Where You Are Called* purposely, for being called is often the way that you discover your path and purpose. You are called to do something; to facilitate a message, house a healing energy, or impart a form of wisdom through sharing your experiences with others.

The call to your path and purpose is often not activated by you alone. The calling is often sent by Source through our own Spiritual Delivery System. The reason for this is that your soul's calling often comes to you in a different form than you may have planned. Many of you shall be surprised by where your soul calls you, but once you are on the path of your true divine calling, always be in reverence of the shape, form and timing it took to place you where you are called to be.

You may find yourself wishing to learn the craft of a particular kind of healing method, without understanding the reason why you are drawn to it. Learn it. Perhaps you begin to experience a certain intuitive ability that you were unaware you possessed. Nurture it. You might feel the desire to travel to a land, a community, or organization that you did not anticipate. Travel there. And then there are some of you that may be spontaneously flung out of your familiar life and into your calling in an instant. Be there.

Regardless of how you answer the call, you may find yourself saying, "This experience is not what I expected or planned for my life. How does this fit in with the big picture?" We suggest that you remain open to all possibilities, for your vision from your place of walking the earthly path is rather limited. The distance of your vision may be short sighted and in this shorter sight of vision, you may have created an alternate and often smaller vision for yourself. Remain open to being called perhaps in a different direction and for a larger purpose than you initially expected. We have the advantage from our location, to see the big picture. Allow us to lead the way. Our system of delivery will always be to your benefit and the benefit of those you serve.

Do not fear that your current abilities and skills may not match this new calling. Your unique gifts will be offered in only a way that you can embody. Know that they will blossom into perfect formation with what you are being called to do. Be open to the common experience of the fact that *all* of your gifts may not have revealed themselves yet. They are on their way. Have patience, for in perfect timing they will be delivered to your door. Fed Ex is not the only service available to deliver your gifts.

And So It Is.

# Teaching 25:
# Practice Non-Attachment

*"A good traveler has no fixed plans,
and is not intent on arriving."*

**Lao Tzu**

THE PRACTICE of non-attachment is a key to advancing your soul. Your soul's nature is to be free. When incarnate in the human body be sure that your soul still yearns for that naturally free state. It is understood that the human experience requires several attachments in order to travel their journey on Earth. Let us suggest some ways to keep both your human self and your soul content.

Your soul needs very little to have a joyful human experience and the less you are attached, the fulfilled you will become internally. You do not own anything. You don't own your spouse, your children, your car, your home, the clothes on your back, or even your physical body. At best, it is all on loan. None of it is truly yours to possess. Ownership of anything that can be seen is unreal. Remain unattached and be free. This is a truth of divine living.

You may at first be fearful while practicing non-attachment. So much of the world and the way humans have set the stage for living is based on the foundation of attachment. You are shown and told from every direction that one must attach and accumulate in order to thrive in the world as a human being. However, attachment often creates more of a human doing than a human being for the accumulation of attachments demands much of your time doing than of being.

Only a few have understood this irony, for the accumulation of the material continues to rise. We speak here of your homes, jobs, bank accounts, clutter, televisions, computers, vehicles, and things you plug in.

Many choose to in fact plug themselves into these things mentioned here to the point that the ability to unplug is forgotten. Allowing yourselves to plug into so many earthly possessions drains the batteries of your energetic systems and often leaves your physical bodies weak and weary.

We do not suggest that you completely detach from all things that are available to you in the physical realm since some of them are good and necessary. We only offer that you use your energies available for attachment wisely. Become discerning about anything you choose to attach to. Your systems were not built to be continuously surrounded with as much noise, static, and images that you take in on a daily basis. For this reason, taking breaks in your time to unplug from these cords that tie you down in the physical world will serve you well. Recharging your physical and spiritual energy systems from time to time will do wonders for your ability to plug in and connect to Source.

In human form this is a challenging task to master since there are many distractions on your planet and plenty to tempt attachment. This often creates a bind and many of you become distracted and attached to worldly possessions of all kinds. This is meant to be, for one of the reasons you are there having a human experience is to literally distract your soul from the memory of who you truly are. The more time that you spend in the daze of who you are not you will eventually yearn to know who you really are. This desire to remember your true being will allow you to begin the art of detachment from some of your worldly possessions. The practice of this will offer a rich experience of returning to the essence of who you were before incarnating.

Let us offer an example of how to practice non-attachment by relating it to the birthing of an idea through inspiration. Inspired ideas are the creation seeds of your outcomes. When these inspirations come to you out of the blue, remember to record them in order to house them in the reality of your physical world. These inspirations come from Spirit and they need to be brought into physical form which requires you to quickly bring that information *into being* by recording it. Practice this when you become inspired.

In that inspiration, or new thought form that has come from Spirit, also practice the art of not attaching to the outcome for it. Be in the inspiration without attachment to its meaning or how you are to create its final form. The steps it takes to create the shape and final formation of the idea into physical reality requires faith on the part of the human self. This requirement of faith is important in that Divine wisdom needs very little assistance. In fact, co-creating with humans, although necessary, can muddy the waters of creative form. Sometimes the human ego will block or at least get in the way of how the creation is to be manifested.

We have the bigger picture and the plan has already been formed, but the outcome is housed in Spirit. It is unnecessary for the human deliverer to be certain of the outcome before it is birthed into earthly existence. The outcome is already perfectly planned, and including plans from ego only delays the manifestation into physical reality.

Ego is the Great Delayer. Ego thinks more of itself than it needs to and will often interfere with the creative process if it is overinvolved. We ask those that are divinely inspired to only do the task that is in front of them, and to only complete the project of that day. To look much further down the path is engaging ego thought forms that may not serve the best and highest purpose of what is being birthed.

Release your grip of attachment to outcomes and remain in the joyful process of co-creation. When inspired, move your ego aside just long enough for the process to unfold with ease and be born in its truest form. Then, once the inspiration is birthed, you will see that it is nothing short of divine perfection.

And So It Is.

# Teaching 26:
# Maintain Balance

"The best and safest thing
is to keep a balance in your life,
acknowledge that great powers are around us
and within us.
Live that way and you are a wise being."


**Euripides**

ONE MUST maintain balance in order to live divinely. The art of balancing in human form is often challenging. As you have noticed, there are many distractions for you in the physical realm. And it is easy to be pulled by those energies that distract and sometimes work to drag you away from your purpose. Staying on your soul's purpose requires balance through physical, emotional, mental, and spiritual discipline. Practicing all four of these disciplines is necessary for complete balance and attunement to occur.

When the physical body is out of balance, maintaining emotional, mental or spiritual balance is nearly impossible. The physical balance of your body is the foundation for all the other systems to even begin working harmoniously. Your discipline of physical balance requires daily attention. Ingestion of clean and regular fuel and maintaining a pattern of sleep that benefits your system and daily movement is necessary. Daily movement is also essential for the body to run at optimal levels as your vehicle. Most of you are neglectful of this foundation of balancing. Know this: When your physical bodies are neglected it is a representation of your neglect on all other levels. Until your body comes into balanced well-being the other systems will remain in at least partial neglect.

The second discipline of learning to maintain balance is housed within your mind. This is the place where most of you have the least amount of discipline regarding all four of your systems. The mind is there to serve you but is often a misguided tool. Your thoughts are not being used in the manner in which they were intended. The mind is a place of much static on your planet. For many of you, your mind is much like that of an undisciplined child.

We understand that in balancing your mind you must also battle the ego and this can be an arduous task. Most of you have nurtured and fed ego to the point where it has taken up residence in your mind filling up most of its space. And ego has no plans of being evicted, but this is what is required. From time to time you have hints, passing moments and sometimes several hours if you are blessed, to experience at least the quieting of the ego's ramblings. It is not ego's place to take over the mind.

Once you begin teaching ego a new way, you may practice the art of discerning ego thoughts from thoughts of your higher Self and higher realms. This is accomplished by quieting the mind as often as time will allow. Quieting the mind is an ability that you all have, but you do not practice. You have worn the strings of the ego's instrument for so long that has become the only song you think you can play. We suggest not only exchanging songs, but changing instruments all together.

Practice this by putting ego aside in the corner or a closet within your mind and begin playing a new song: a song of silence. By stilling the waters of your mind you will begin to hear another voice, the voice you have been neglecting. This is the voice of your soul. We offer silence as the discipline for the mind. It is required to come into balance and will take practice.

The third discipline is that of your emotional system and the balancing of your two emotions. We are speaking here of fear and love. Coming into balance with these two emotions does not suggest that you should feel them both equally. There is very little fear that actually needs to be felt. It is of minimal requirement and is only there to serve the purpose of keeping you physically in your body. At all other times, coming into balance with your emotional system, we suggest spending most of it in love. It is that simple.

The fourth discipline is the discipline of connecting to Source through your spiritual life. You return to the discipline of your spiritual life by using your tools and rituals to maintain your daily practice. Maintaining the discipline and practice of connecting to Source will bring you into balance. Notice we did not suggest practicing *another's* spiritual discipline. Practice only your own. Spend time connecting in the ways that are meaningful only for you, for that is the only way you will come into contact with your own divinity.

In order to truly embrace your divinity in human form, balance is required. Balancing through these four disciplines will become more natural for you over time, as everything that you practice does. Once this becomes a way of being, your connection will become stronger and you will walk your path with greater ease and lightness.

In living your lives, notice each of these four areas. Where in your life are you are not disciplined? Where in these four areas do you need to concentrate your efforts and bring yourself back to a place of harmony and well-being? Practicing these four disciplines will require slight variations, for each of you and your systems are unique unto themselves. As you are coming to know each of these systems that we are discussing here today about balance-your physical, emotional, mental and spiritual well-being, you are learning which ones are off kilter.

Go to those places that are unstable within you, or have been neglected and work to restore harmony. And then maintain that harmony through your practices and rituals as you spend time throughout your day. From the gift of natural balance that you will be giving to yourselves you will also receive the gift of peace.

And So It Is.

# Teaching 27:
# Breathe in the Aroma of Creation

"And the day came
when the risk to remain tight in a bud
was more painful than the risk
it took to blossom."

**Anais Nin**

WATER YOUR garden of divine creation daily. Creating is what you are doing in human form. You are a Universal creation and will return to your Creator when you decide this chapter of the journey is complete. Until that glorious day, nurture and care for the seeds of creativity within your garden.

Do so first by planting them in fertile soil. The seeds of creative power have always resided inside of you, although some of you were not truly ready to recognize it until now. This creative part of yourself has been waiting for you to believe in yourself so that its seeds may be planted. For some it is difficult to embrace your creativity. Some of you have been turning your back on this part of you for so long, refusing to water the soil that houses your creative seeds. This fertile space that was birthed with you in human form is often neglected to the point that it becomes as dry and cracked as the desert floor. To those who know this as your truth, you have ignored your creative essence long enough.

Turn around towards your creative gifts once again. Each of you has exquisite creative gardens within just waiting to be planted. Awaken to the divine creative energies of this life path. Overturn a new bed of creative soil housed inside your divine being. Build new fertile ground and transform what was once dry arid soil to return it to its original form. Now plant the first seed and clearly see the bud of this first flower. Offer this bud your divine drops of inspiration. Together with the sunlight and fresh air, you will begin deepening its roots.

Continue to embrace your creative energy and watch it grow, forming rich green leaves. You will soon witness your bud beginning to bloom. This is the first flower of your new garden of creation.

Tend to your creation daily as the aroma from this flower begins to become known to you. Breathe in the unique scent this flower offers to you as a gift. Through your breath, the vapors from the swelling aroma will imprint in your mind to keep you connected. As you breathe in this sweet scent, bring it down now into your core and through the channel that connects with Mother Earth. Doing so will root each flower in strength planting it firmly in sacred ground. Finally breathe it deeply into your heart. It is from within your heart that you will witness the full blossom manifesting into physical form.

This is how to breathe in your own aroma of creation. Use this visualization to connect and enhance your own creative process from the beginnings of inspiration to the outcome of a magical manifestation. This is for all who are now in the process, and also for those who are becoming ready to plant, germinate, grow and blossom a divine creation.

The power of the creative Spirit is within each one of you. You can all create new life in many splendid forms. Plant your seed in fertile soil. Ground it in the wisdom and patience of Mother Earth. Water each bud with your divine drops of inspiration. Offer your encouragement with pure intention while it grows within your heart. And as you witness it bloom, feed it daily with your divine breath of these four words: "I believe in you."

And So It Is.

# Teaching 28:
# Express Yourself

"The universe must exist for the
self-expression of God
and the delight of God."

**Ernest Holmes**

TO WALK the path of life as the truly divine being that you are, you must believe this truth: You are an expression of God. And in that expression we offer this teaching to you so that you may express yourselves in the image, memory and knowing that you are God expressing God Itself. Each of God's unique features is embodied within each one of your thoughts, words, and deeds.

We will begin with your thought forms for they are generally the way that you embody your initial expressions. These thoughtful expressions are distinctive unto you, for they house your unique historical memories from this lifetime. They also house memories of your dream time as well as dreams in the form of what you aspire to be and do. As you now know, your thought forms also house your ego. We suggest you find a small corner for your ego within your mind and house it there. We make this suggestion, for it is your ego that can constantly attempt to express itself through your lower thought forms in ways that may not serve your higher purpose.

Choose only the dreams, aspirations and thought forms that represent the true expression of who you are. And yes, you do have choice. You have the ability to be discerning of your own thoughts. Bring forth only the thoughts that you wish to express in your words and deeds. Pay little attention to the others, for they are likely not to be your truth and will not support your purpose.

The second more potent way of expressing yourself is with your words because your voice can be heard outside the realm of your private mind by others in your presence. The expression of your voice is a creative tool that carries a powerful vibrational energy. Each word that you speak resonates not just within your own body, but also travels into the energetic field of others that hear you. And if they choose to resonate with your words, they will pull them from their vibrational energy field, housing them within their own bodies.

Therefore your words have the power to resonate with others who also recognize your words as their truth. This forms a powerful connection between the truth spoken by the deliverer and the truth that resonates within the receiver. Your words are your Great Expressions. Choose them wisely and share them with only those whom you feel called to connect with consciously.

In choosing your words, pause and ask yourself three questions: "Is this my truth? Is this necessary to share now? What impact might they have on another?" And if the answer to the third question, at least from your knowing, is one of negativity and does not come from a thought born in love, we suggest you pause, and return to the second question, "Is this necessary to share now?" And if it is not necessary, then remaining quiet may be the best choice.

The third form of human expression is that of your deeds. If you have chosen you thoughts and words carefully and consciously, these deeds are the most powerful tool of expression you have available to you. In combination with thought and word, action taken from those two former expressions can do great things. Your actions are the Great Transformers. They are the expressions of yourself that demonstrate who you believe yourself to be. Your actions have the ability to transform not only your own lives, but also the lives of others.

This is a great responsibility and is not to be taken lightly, for your actions can not only change and transform yourselves and others for the good, they can also do irreparable damage when used without consciousness or pure heart-full intention. Before acting on your thoughts and words, we suggest that you pause to ask, "Is this action born out of my truthful thoughts and words?" If the answer is clearly yes, then ask, "What active expression am I now ready to perform?"

Do not go blindly into action. Your heart must be willing to take that journey with you, for it is your heart that will keep you in your truth. If your heart is ready, only take those action steps that are true representations and real expression of your soul. This is important since action is expression in motion, vibrating at a very powerful frequency and cannot be retracted. We offer that you chose only the actions that are your true external expressions of love.

Expressing yourself on all three levels is a true gift that you have as humans. Recognize their power and use them consciously. Before you choose to express, always pause to listen to the wisdom within. You are all powerful creators manifesting the unique expressions of yourselves at all times and for all time. Your soul's power through your human tools of expression can manifest miracles in the expression of love, and also manifest destruction in the expression of fear. Remember that any form of destruction is birthed from fear. It begins with a fearful thought in the mind, and does not take long to manifest into words followed by deeds. The power to destroy through fear is a choice for all humans, for it comes attached to the gift of free will.

When choosing to express yourself let your ultimate question be: "Will I choose an expression of love or an expression of fear?" Go forth with this freedom, and through your thoughts, words, and deeds, express only love. Love is the most powerful, miraculous expression there is, for it is the only purely truthful expression of God. You can begin to practice this expression by declaring the following statements. Over time, through the form of repetition, you will come to believe and embody your soul's divinity:

I am abundant, I am accepting, I am affirming, I am ageless,
I am alive, I am allowing, I am authentic, I am awake,
I am balanced, I am being, I am birthing, I am blessed,
I am bountiful, I am centered, I am changing,
I am complete, I am connected, I am conscious,
I am creating, I am detached, I am divine, I am embodied,
I am endless, I am enlightened, I am eternal, I am evolving,
I am expanding, I am expressive, I am extraordinary,
I am flowing, I am forgiving, I am free, I am fulfilled,
I am genuine, I am giving, I am good, I am grateful,
I am growing, I am healthy, I am here, I am humble,
I am illuminated, I am incarnate, I am infinite, I am
inspired, I am intelligent, I am intuitive, I am joyful, I am kind,
I am knowing, I am liberating, I am listening, I am loving,
I am magnificent, I am manifesting, I am masterful,
I am meaningful, I am meditative, I am miraculous,
I am moderate, I am moving, I am natural, I am necessary,

I am now, I am nurturing, I am offering, I am one,
I am open, I am original, I am peaceful, I am perfect,
I am playful, I am powerful, I am present, I am purposeful,
I am radiant, I am realizing, I am receiving, I am relational,
I am remembering, I am renewed, I am sacred, I am
serving, I am silent, I am soulful, I am source, I am spontaneous,
I am still, I am supporting, I am timeless, I am
transcendent, I am transforming, I am trusting, I am truthful,
I am unconditional, I am unique, I am united, I am universal,
I am unlimited, I am visionary, I am vital, I am well,
I am whole, I am willing, I am wise, I am within,
I am wondrous, I am yielding,
I am.

And So It Is.

# Teaching 29:
# Remember We Are One

"When you're inspired,
you remember that God is always in you
and you're always in God,
so you're incapable of thinking
limited thoughts."

**Wayne Dyer**

WE ARE all One. We are all connected. There is no true form of what you call disconnection or separation. We are all divine beings having experiences in this moment of now. We are all present for all time and we all come together as we always have and always will be, connected for all time as One. We are all coming from Source and all returning to Source, and all experiencing Source now, for now is all there is or ever was. There is no past or future, there is only the divine present moment.

As humans, your beliefs in the thought forms of the past and of a so called future are concepts you have imagined. They are not real. The time of life is always now and takes the formation of a spiral instead of your linear line. The spiral of now is spinning throughout all the ages, and all the creations, and all the planets, and all the creatures, and all the beings that ever were, are, and shall be. We are all spinning our own unique threads on this spiral in connection to all that is: the Divine One.

Each of our beings represents a thread and together we are connected and woven together to make up the entire fabric of the one entity and energy that is God. This fabric is infinite. It has no edges. It has no place where it ends, for it has no place where it is not. It has no place where the threads are cut or disconnected. And your divine spiraling thread is never misguided and will never go missing from the fabric it belongs to, for God is infinitely everywhere, connecting always in the now through each thread for the purpose of experiencing all of Itself.

You could never be misplaced because separation is not part of the divine plan for it serves no purpose. You are all divinely woven into your perfect place, spiraling in connection with your human body in this lifetime and also with all of your other lifetimes within your thread. You are always blending with all of your lives threading through the spiral now.

Each of us offers a perfect and unique aspect of God that God desires to remember. And your unique thread is woven into the fabric always on purpose. You are a part of God that no other thread woven within the one infinite fabric can create. You are the exact memory of that part of God in the perfect form that only you can be. And you are necessary, as necessary as any of the other threads woven into the fabric, for your thread completes the fabric and without you God would be missing a part of God's Self. And God missing a part of Itself is the only impossibility in the universe. God is always complete.

And together, the chorus of our voices is singing one song in perfect harmony. All of us have come into formation so that we may each sing a chord of the only song that has ever been sung: The Song of Life. And each of our chords vibrate together to form the divine frequency of Love. For love is the only divine frequency that our true voices ever resonate with, bringing us all into harmony as we sing one song called Life.

Some of you in your spiraling threads are in human form for God wishes to know itself within the formation of human experience. Then there are those of us within the fabric that represents God having an experience in Spirit form. Both in flesh and in Spirit we are all combined together to complete the formation of the fabric of God.

You are currently in human form as God resonating within each breath that you take. You are God in formation choosing to be on Earth at this time with all others who walk the planet now for one collective purpose. You have chosen to bring forth the great awakening and to speak the truth that has been forgotten: We Are One. Any human belief or communication that is not in harmony with these three words is not the Truth. It is time to communicate and reconnect with this truth.

From all that we have offered through our teachings, if there was only one word that our collective Soul could communicate for all teachings that ever were, ever are, and ever shall be, it would culminate them all into this word: One. Go forth to share this with all who are ready, for it is the only word ever needed to illuminate the soul's purpose for being.

And So It Is.

# Teaching 30:
# Go Silently Within

"God cannot be found in noise and restlessness.
God is the friend of silence.
See how nature grows in silence; see the stars,
the moon and the sun, how
they move in silence.
We need silence to be able to touch souls."

Mother Teresa

THE VOICE of God is heard most clearly in quiet moments, for silence is the language of God. If you wish for these teachings to begin to settle inside you, become willing and able to spend time in solitude and silence.

And So It Is.

# Final Offering from Magdalene

ADVANCING YOUR soul is what you are doing here. In order to remember this, you must keep that soul memory alive with your daily relationship to the Divine. Spending time in conscious connection is the only lasting way to embrace your divine soul and marry it to your earthly journey. This is what we have been showing you along the journey.

You all have the gracious opportunity to do so, yet many still choose to walk unconscious. If you truly commit to engaging with the Divine on an ongoing basis, you will awaken and be able to consciously enjoy spending your earthly time doing what you showed up to do. Therefore, Divine Engagements are a final tool we offer for your ongoing practice to keep the teachings fresh and they are another way to truly make a daily commitment to your own divinity.

Each morning ask Divine Spirit for assistance in choosing one of the following engagements and commit to complete the task it offers within that day. Then watch for the perfect circumstances, people and opportunities show up to assist you in completing the engagement. Commit to the activity for as long as possible each day in order to truly engage with the Divine. And remember to always enjoy and have fun, since that's what being Divine in human formation is all about!

# Divine Engagements

- ★ Activate, announce, and embrace your unique Spirit name.
- ★ Take a media holiday.
- ★ Join or participate in a cause to Re-cover Mother Earth.
- ★ Meditate.
- ★ Make an anonymous donation.
- ★ Reach out to someone you have missed in your life with the intention to reconnect.
- ★ Create and state your daily intention.
- ★ Create a 24 hour no complaint zone in your home.
- ★ Watch spiritual cinema.
- ★ Spend time walking outdoors.
- ★ Read spiritual literature.
- ★ Record an exhaustive list of all thing in your life for which you are currently grateful.
- ★ Move your body.
- ★ Take yourself on a play date.
- ★ Release 3 items from your home or office that no longer serve you.
- ★ Repeat your Divine Declaration as a mantra throughout your day as often as possible.
- ★ Find a love song that resonates for you and play it in dedication to yourself.
- ★ Spend time with a creature from the animal kingdom.
- ★ Create a 24 hour no gossip zone in your home or office.

- ★ Lay under the night sky and watch the stars.
- ★ Speak only kind words to others all day long.
- ★ Send a silent blessing to all those you interact with today.
- ★ Spend time automatic writing in your journal.
- ★ Write 10 old beliefs you have about the Divine Creator and reframe all that are not true for you.
- ★ Communicate with an object in nature.
- ★ In the presence of anyone today who is speaking negatively about another, defend the absent.
- ★ Bless every morsel of food and drop of water you intake today.
- ★ Listen for your own negative thoughts and instantly offer a positive reframe.
- ★ Do one thing outside your comfort zone today.
- ★ Write in detail about a personal experience when you felt love.
- ★ Tell a family member or loved one "thank you for being in my life."
- ★ Have a TV free day.
- ★ Write 10 old beliefs you have about yourself and reframe all that are not true.
- ★ Take a friend or companion on a play date.
- ★ Define one thing that you are afraid of currently and take action towards overcoming the fear.

* Recycle all possible items you use today.
* Scan for the positive in your life all day and record each one throughout your day.
* Spend 30 minutes gathering items in a box for donation and drop it off.
* Participate in an activity of your choice that makes you laugh.
* Give 30 minutes of your time to someone in need today.
* Record as many positive attributes about yourself as possible.
* Write your current bucket list and make a concrete plan for at least one of them.
* Pray/send blessings to one person your dislike or resent.
* Write a mission statement for your life's purpose and post it on your bathroom mirror.
* Conserve as much water as possible in your home/office today.
* Do one thing today to reduce your carbon footprint.
* Spend 30 waking minutes in complete silence today.
* Put only life enhancing substances in your body today.
* Create a visualization to connect with Source and take time to do so today.
* Find a peaceful resolution to a current conflict and commit to resolve it.

* Think of someone you know who is struggling in their life and send them a card of encouragement.
* Tell a child today that you believe in them.
* Unplug from one of your technologies for 24 hours.
* Write an appreciation letter to yourself for your dedication to growth and mail it to yourself.
* Replace two light bulbs in your home with energy saving light bulbs.
* Tell three strangers to have a beautiful day.
* Record the story of your return to Spirit and how you imagine the experience.
* Spend time in a creative activity of your choice.
* Do one thing to enhance your physical well-being today.
* Tell someone you love them and why.
* Do one thing, that if left undone, you will eventually regret.
* Recognize the Divine in every person you meet today.
* Spend 30 minutes in complete solitude today.
* Place yourself at the top of your priority list today.
* Call on a being from your heavenly support team to co-create something with you.
* Perform a random act of kindness for a stranger.

* Listen to only positive uplifting music today.
* Say no or cancel one engagement that drains your energy.
* Write a letter to someone on the planet who does not enjoy freedom.
* Take the day off.
* Remove one thing from your environment or life that is toxic.
* Try something brand new today that you have never done before but wanted to.
* Draw a picture or write a poem describing how you experience the Divine.
* Sit completely still in a comfortable chair for 30 minutes.
* Speak only kind and positive words about yourself today.
* Do one activity today to raise your planetary consciousness.
* Spend 30 minutes in a natural setting and record your feelings.
* Write your eulogy of what you hope to be said about your life.
* Take one step towards your true life purpose today.
* Make an amends for a recent behavior.
* Do one thing in your community today to promote peace.
* Ask someone for help today.
* Practice a meaningful connection with Mother Earth.

* In response to any anger you encounter from another today return only love.
* Record all the ways this world is a better place with you in it.
* Describe to someone why it is important to be on the planet at this time in evolution.
* Find as many opportunities as possible and work on downsizing your ego today.
* Notice all the ways abundance flows into your life today.
* Record all the current challenges in your life today, read aloud and then thank each one of them.
* Build an altar in your home, and if you already have one, create another.
* Admit a part of your shadow to yourself and write an acceptance letter to that part of yourself.
* Call on someone from your earthly support team to co-create something with you.
* Notice one way you disconnect from Source and find a way to reconnect.
* Educate yourself about the life story and impact of an ascended divine being of your choice.
* Spend 30 minutes sending blessings of peace to humanity.
* Introduce yourself to someone new today.
* Release one worldly possession that you are attached to.

* Notice your thoughts and words of discrimination today and commit to thoughts and words of equality.
* Visit a graveyard and share your experience with someone.
* Write how you wish to spend the rest of your time here on Earth and share it with someone.
* Host a celebration party in honor of being Divine.
* Practice non-attachment to any outcomes today.
* Tell your truth all day long.
* Find a way to be of service to someone that you judge.
* Bring live flowers or a live plant into your home.
* Thank the universe in advance for something you wish to manifest in your life.
* Plan a gathering for an activity that will raise the collective consciousness of the planet.
* Spend time in water today and create a ritual for blessing the water.
* Send morning and evening salutations to the Sun today for its life giving energy.
* Rewind to the time before your birth and describe what your plan was for this lifetime.
* Create your own Divine Engagement.

# In Closing

I am grateful to Mary Magdalene for teaching me how to advance my soul and embrace my own divine nature. I also give thanks to those who are reading this message. If the words within these pages have touched your heart, I invite you to share them with other souls you meet along the way. And always trust your divine wisdom within, for you are the miraculous manifestation of all that is, ever was, and ever shall be. Go forth in the loving memory of this truth: We Are One.

Your messenger,

*Eva Rose.*

# About the Author

Eva spent twenty years as a psychotherapist assisting others in understanding the reasons why their lives were off track and how to align with their true purpose. She began writing about her own process of transformation after a spontaneous spiritual awakening dramatically altered the course of her life. She is the author of two books, *A Guide for Advancing Your Soul*, and *The 30 Teachings of Mary Magdalene*. Eva holds a Master's degree and is currently a doctoral candidate in the field of human services. To share her inspirational message, she spends time speaking and conducting workshops around the globe and resides in Arizona with her family.